U0935215

中国-东盟
命运共同体与澜湄合作

——第九届西南论坛暨第二届澜湄合作智库论坛论文集

Lancang-Mekong Cooperation and A Community of Shared Future for China-ASEAN:

The 9th Southwest Forum and the 2nd Lancang-Mekong Cooperation Think Tank Forum

林文勋　郑永年 ◎ 主编

社会科学文献出版社
SOCIAL SCIENCES ACADEMIC PRESS (CHINA)

主办方 云南大学
大理大学
新加坡国立大学东亚研究所

承办方 云南大学周边外交研究中心
大理面向南亚东南亚辐射中心（澜湄合作）研究院

2018 年 9 月 25～28 日　中国·大理

前　言

习近平主席指出，中国和东盟国家山水相连，血脉相亲，是好邻居、好朋友、好伙伴。自 20 世纪 90 年代以来，中国同东盟关系持续快速发展。2003 年 10 月，在第七次中国－东盟领导人会议上，双方宣布建立面向和平与繁荣的战略伙伴关系，开启了中国－东盟友好关系的新篇章。2013 年 10 月，习近平主席在访问印尼时提出愿同东盟国家共建“21 世纪海上丝绸之路”，携手建设更为紧密的中国－东盟命运共同体。由此，“一带一路”倡议与命运共同体的理念同时为中国－东盟关系发展勾画了美好蓝图。

2018 年，是中国－东盟建立战略伙伴关系 15 周年，也是“一带一路”倡议提出 5 周年。在过去的 15 年里，中国与东盟的友谊之树根深叶茂、互利合作硕果累累。特别是在“一带一路”倡议提出 5 年来，双方弘扬丝路精神，在携手构建中国 - 东盟命运共同体道路上，迈出了更加坚实的步伐。一是战略合作日益紧密。中国始终把东盟作为周边外交的优先方向，支持东盟共同体的建设和东盟在区域合作中的中心地位，同时东盟国家将中国视为值得信赖的合作伙伴。双方通过在东盟与中日韩（10 +3）合作、东亚峰会、东盟地区论坛、亚太经合组织等合作机制中开展全方位、多层次、宽领域的对话交流，增进政治互信，聚焦合作发展，维护地区和平、发展与繁荣。经受住了时间考验的中国 - 东盟合作关系，已经成为亚太区域合作中最为成功和最具活力的典范。二是开放合作全面深化。中国率先同东盟商谈并在 2010 年建成了中国 - 东盟自由贸易区。东盟是“一带一路”国际合作的优先方向和重要伙伴。截止到 2018 年，中国已连续 9 年成为东盟第一大贸易伙伴，东盟连续 7 年成为中国第三大贸易伙伴。中国与东盟双向投资额累计超过了 2000 亿美元，中国在东盟设立直接投资企业 4000 余家，雇用当地员工 30 多万人，有力地促进了当地经济社会发展。三是人文合作蓬勃发展。双方成功举办了科技、文化、海洋、教育、旅游等主题年活动，2018 年又启动了中国 - 东盟创新年。2017 年双向人员往来近 5000 万人次，双方互派留学生超过 20 万人。中国在东盟国家设立了 6 个文化中心、33 个孔子学院、35 个孔子课堂。当前，中国 - 东盟战略伙伴关系正以政治安全、经贸、人文交流三大支柱为主线，多领域合作为支持的“3 + X 合作框架”得到推进，中国 - 东盟命运共同体的实践内涵被不断丰富。

而作为东盟与中国地缘相近、人文相亲优势凸显的重要组成部分，澜湄次区域是中国和东盟之间的陆上连接枢纽，也是“一带一路”的交叉结合区域，在中国 - 东盟的合作中存在更坚实的经济、政治、安全、人文和生态领域合作基础。2015 年 11 月，中国和湄公河国家老、柬、泰、缅、越五国建立了弥补既有机制不足的全新经济合作框架——澜沧江 - 湄公河对话合作机制，并在 2016 年 3 月首次澜湄合作领导人会议上发表了《三亚宣言》，确定了六国合作发展的“3 + 5”框架，即以政治 - 安全、经济和可持续发展、社会 - 人文为三大合作支柱，优先在互联互通、产能合作、跨境经济、水资源、农业和减贫领域开展合作。在成立 3 年多来，澜湄合作机制化日趋成熟，建立了领导人会议、外长会、高官会和各领域的工作组会等四个层次的机制，六国先后设立了澜湄合作国家秘书处、水资源合作中心等协调机构；完成或实质开展了首次领导人会议确定的 45 个早收项目和第二次外长会中方提出的 13 个倡议中的大部分；保障了项目合作资金，促进 3 亿美元的澜湄合作专项基金和 50 亿美元产能合作专项贷款等资金投入到位，向世界展现了“澜湄效率”和六国以合作促发展的决心。2018 年 1 月，第二次澜湄合作领导人会议提出了系统涵盖澜湄合作目标、准则、架构、领域和体系的《澜湄合作五年行动计划(2018—2022)》和“3+5+X”的合作框架，各国致力于共建澜湄流域经济发展带，这标志着澜湄合作从“培育期”进入了“成长期”。山水相连、经济互补、人文相通的澜湄各国间，更具备了实现澜湄国家命运共同体的坚实基础。按照王毅外长的说法，澜湄六国已经确定了“本着平等协商的精神，致力于维护地区和平稳定，缩小发展差距，携手打造团结互助、平等协商、互惠互利、合作共赢的澜湄国家命运共同体”的共识。由此，以澜湄合作为基础的澜湄国家命运共同体作为首个得到相关国家正式认可且已进入建设议程的命运共同体，已成为构建人类命运共同体先行先试的高阶基础和重点方向。

中国改革开放40年来的经验表明，开放是促进发展的巨大动力，对发展相对滞后的西南地区来说更是如此。党的十九大报告明确提出，要推动形成全面开放新格局，要以“一带一路”建设为重点，坚持引进来和走出去并重，遵循共商共建共享原则，加强创新能力开放合作，形成陆海内外联动、东西双向互济的开放格局。西南地区凭借紧邻东盟的区位优势和国家西部大开发战略赋予的体制机制优势，已成为发展中国-东盟战略伙伴关系、参与澜湄合作等次区域合作的前沿。当前，西南地区正积极推动内陆和沿边地区的开发开放，通过“面向南亚东南亚辐射中心”“南向通道”的规划建设，主动融入和服务于“一带一路”和国家周边外交战略。这是实施开放促发展战略的必然要求，也是西南地区彰显自身诸多优势的时代契机。而在当前国际政治经济局势变革与风险并存的背景下，西南地区如何在把握国家战略布局新取向的基础上，在经济发展新旧动能转换的过程中充分发挥自身优势、释放合作开放潜力以实现社会经济跨越式发展，将是长期面临的重点和难题。

“西南论坛”创办于2010年，经过9年的发展，已经成为中国西南地区层次最高、影响最广的学术论坛之一。西南论坛每年举办一次，主要设置有关国家战略推进和区域经济社会发展中的重大理论和实践议题，吸引国内外众多相关领域权威专家、学者的参与，搭建起了西南地区与国际学术界接轨的桥梁。2018年时值中国－东盟建立战略合作伙伴关系15周年，“一带一路”倡议提出5周年，也是澜沧江－湄公河合作从培育期进入成长期的关键年份，为进一步探究中国－东盟命运共同体构建视角下中国与东南亚国家关系发展存在的机遇与挑战，分析中国周边外交与安全中的关键因素和热点问题对构建新型周边关系的影响，探讨澜湄合作从培育期进入成长期后的发展重点与推进路径，总结中国西南地区参与“一带一路”建设和面向东南亚的区域合作进程和经验，云南大学周边外交研究中心与新加坡国立大学东亚研究所、大理面向南亚东南亚辐射中心（澜湄合作）研究院于2018年9月26～27日在云南大理联合举办了“第九届西南论坛暨第二届澜湄合作智库论坛”。

此次论坛的主题是“中国－东盟命运共同体与澜湄合作”，论坛设置了“人类命运共同体与中国－东盟命运共同体”“新型国际关系与新型周边关系”“从培育期进入成长期的澜湄合作”“经济走廊与澜湄发展走廊”等四个主要议题。与会代表深入开展了思想交流与智慧碰撞，积极响应了时代主题，从历史和现实的双重维度出发，进一步厘清了人类命运共同体与中国－东盟命运共同体之间的关系，探讨了中国－东盟合作的新方向和澜湄合作进入成长期后的建设路径，对在“一带一路”建设和周边外交开展的实质性问题进行了深入的剖析，提出了不少具有高水平、高质量的学术观点与政策建议，为推进“一带一路”建设、西南地区的发展、构建全面开放新格局，为打造更紧密的中国－东盟命运共同体、探索构建人类命运共同体在周边的先行先试，提供重要的理论和策略参考。

为充分展示与会专家、学者在本届论坛上的真知灼见以及当前他们的前沿研究成果，本论文集共整理收录了13篇有代表性的参会论文，以飨读者。

林文勋　郑永年

2019年6月18日

目　录

主旨演讲

人类命运共同体与中国 - 东盟命运共同体

新型国际关系与新型周边关系

从培育期进入成长期的澜湄合作

经济走廊与澜湄发展走廊

主旨演讲

以智慧促合作助力构建中国-东盟命运共同体

杨　林*

尊敬的黄毅副主席、管木大使、朱成虎将军、段林书记，

尊敬的各位领导、各位专家，女士们、先生们、朋友们，大家上午好！

很高兴与大家汇聚在美丽的风花雪月之乡大理，共同出席第九届西南论坛暨第二届澜湄合作智库论坛。首先，我谨代表云南大学，对本次论坛的召开表示热烈祝贺！对与会的各位专家学者和嘉宾朋友们表示热烈的欢迎！

白驹过隙，时光荏苒。西南论坛自 2010 年首次举办，到 2018 年已经是第九届。几年来，在各位朋友和有关单位的关

---

* 杨林，中共云南省委高校工委常务副书记，时任云南大学党委书记、教授。

心支持下，西南论坛已经逐渐成为国内知名、享誉东南亚的高端论坛，成为云南大学国际问题研究和国际交流的亮丽名片，为促进中国－东盟友好合作和学术交流做出了积极的贡献。本届论坛是由云南大学、大理大学以及新加坡国立大学东亚研究所共同主办，由云南大学周边外交研究中心、大理面向南亚东南亚辐射中心（澜湄合作）研究院具体承办。论坛获得了莅临现场的各兄弟单位和领导专家的鼎力支持，在此，我代表云南大学致以衷心的感谢！

中国与东盟山水相连，是好邻居、好朋友、好伙伴。2013年10月，习近平主席在访问印尼时提出，中国愿同东盟兴衰相伴、安危与共、同舟共济，携手建设更为紧密的中国－东盟命运共同体。在去年召开的中国共产党十九大报告中，习总书记明确了新时代中国外交要推动构建新型国际关系，推动构建人类命运共同体的任务。在2018年6月中央外事工作会议上，习总书记更提出了以促进民族复兴、人类进步为主线，推动构建人类命运共同体的总要求。因此，在2018年中国－东盟建立战略合作伙伴关系15周年，也是澜沧江－湄公河合作从培育期进入成长期的关键节点之际，本届论坛以“中国－东盟命运共同体与澜湄合作”为主题，从历史和现实的双重维度出发，总结展望中国－东盟合作的新方向，探讨进入成长期后澜湄合作的建设路径。论坛主要将围绕“人类命运共同体与中国－东盟命运共同体”“新型国际关系与新型周边关系”“从培育期进入成长期的澜湄合作”“经济走廊与澜湄发展走廊”等多项议题展开深入研讨。因此，本届论坛对于践行党的十九大报告精神和习近平新时代中国特色社会主义外交思想、发展与周边国家关系、打造中国－东盟更高水平的战略伙伴关系、迈向更为紧密的中国－东盟命运共同体、探索构建人类命运共同体的先行先试有所讨论，具有重要的学术价值与现实意义。

作为国家首批“双一流大学”建设高校之一，云南大学紧紧围绕建设世界一流大学目标，主动融入国家战略，积极服务云南经济社会发展，遵循“开放合作、集成创新、协调共进、特色发展”的发展理念，按照立足云南、服务国家、辐射两亚、走向世界的办学思路，着力从四个方面大力推动规划和实施“双一流大学”的建设过程。

第一，多措并举服务国家需求。近年来，我校主动融入和服务国家战略，开展了多项富有成效的实践工作。先前“中缅油气管道与中国能源安全”“西南国际河流与跨境生态安全”等原创性成果为国家提供了决策参考；2015 年 12 月，科技部与云南省人民政府联合发文，批准依托云南大学与云南农业大学共建云南生物资源保护与利用国家重点实验室；2016 年起我校承担了《习近平谈治国理政》一书缅甸、老挝、尼泊尔、孟加拉国和印度等五国语言的翻译、出版和推广工作；此外我校还着力推进“树木树人计划”“云南大学服务云南行动计划”等。尤其是在 2018 年 7 月 14 日，中国高等教育学会

“一带一路”研究分会在我校成立，这为云大站在新的历史起点，充分发挥自身地理区位优势，助推国家“一带一路”建设、推动高等教育开放和促进高等教育国际交流与合作，提供了新的历史机遇与要求。

第二，多管齐下打造优势学科。2015 年 1 月，习近平总书记在云南考察工作时指出，希望云南主动服务和融入国家发展战略，闯出一条跨越式发展的路子来，努力成为民族团结进步示范区、生态文明建设排头兵、面向南亚东南亚辐射中心，谱写好中国梦的云南篇章。而云南大学目前已经形成的以民族学、生物学、特色资源开发与环境保护，以及边疆问题和东南亚、南亚国际问题研究为优势特色的学科体系，能够积极服务于云南的三大定位建设。同时，学校通过大力实施“学术兴校”战略，科学研究水平显著提升。在最近一轮教育部学科评估中，云大的民族学、生态学排名第二，政治学排名第六；微生物学、化学学科进入 ESI 全球前 1%。自然科学领域，新增科技创新平台 17 个，实现国家重点实验室、国际联合实验室、国家技术转移示范中心零的突破。

第三，多方努力构建人才高地。在本月刚结束的全国教育大会上，习总书记强调，要坚持把学校教师队伍建设作为基础工作予以重视。当前，云南大学正大力实施“人才强校”战略，构建以科学评价、人尽其才为核心的人才队伍体系，建设高水平人才队伍。目前，已新增“千人计划”“长江学者”

“杰青”“优青”等高层次人才 10 人，总数达 15 人，较 2011 年数量增长 2 倍。新增云南省科技领军人才 5 人、“云岭学者”13 人，遴选特聘教授 26 人、青年英才 49 人、“东陆中青年骨干教师”300 余人，师资队伍数量稳步增长，质量显著提升，结构更趋合理。

第四，多校合作迈向国际化。云南大学充分发挥区位优势，全面加强与南亚东南亚国家的大学合作办学。孔子学院建设成效显著，目前总数已达 4 所。学校被国家汉办批准为“一带一路”南亚东南亚国家汉语推广基地，圆满承办了第十一届全球孔子学院大会。目前，云南大学作为大湄公河次区域的两个高校联盟组织“大湄公河次区域高等教育联合会”及“大湄公河次区域学术研究网络”的理事单位，积极拓展了与湄公河国家高校的交流与合作，已经与湄公河流域国家的 20 多所高校和机构建立了合作关系。今后，云大将继续发挥云南省毗邻缅甸、老挝、泰国、柬埔寨、越南等国家的地理位置优势，通过实施“南亚东南亚大学联盟”计划、“留学云南大学计划”等举措，成为南亚东南亚学生出国留学首选目的地，建成全国规模最大、体系最为完备的南亚东南亚区域国别研究基地，大踏步迈向国际化。

云南大学的国际关系学科是我校一直着力推动的重点学科，更是“云南大学一流大学建设方案”中“边疆治理与地缘政治学科群”下的重要组成部分。国际关系学科现已建成国内最全的“一带一路”沿线国家区域国别研究体系，聚焦边疆治理与地缘政治中的重大理论和现实问题，致力于“一带一路”与新地缘政治学、周边外交理论与实践创新等重点领域的研究，并成为全国国际关系拔尖创新人才培养重镇，在边疆治理和地缘政治领域形成具有中国特色、中国风格、中国气派的学术体系和话语体系，全面服务于我国边疆治理、周边外交和中国面向南亚东南亚辐射中心建设。

与此同时，云南大学积极响应国家加强中国特色新型智库建设的号召，重点支持周边外交研究中心的发展，努力将其建设成为教育部新型高校智库或重点研究基地。中心建设至今，在推动国内外学术交流、社会科学专题数据库建设等方面取得了积极进展。这些成绩的取得，离不开包括在座各位的专家学者和兄弟单位的大力关心和鼎力支持，在此我代表云南大学再次致以诚挚的谢意。谢谢你们！

女士们、先生们，朋友们！

十五载中国－东盟战略合作休戚与共，九届西南论坛智慧共享。希望西南论坛作为一年一度的学术盛会，能够进一步夯实交流对话平台，拓宽智库合作渠道，为推动中国－东盟友好合作再上新台阶做出更大贡献。最后，预祝第九届西南论坛暨第二届澜湄合作智库论坛取得完满成功！祝各位来宾在大理期间身心愉快、身体健康！

谢谢大家！

澜湄合作：进展与趋势

刘　稚*

摘　要： 2017年以来，澜沧江-湄公河合作在中方的积极推动和相关各国的共同努力下，各方在政治安全、经济和可持续发展、社会人文三大支柱和互联互通、产能、跨境经济、水资源、农业和减贫五个优先领域的合作都取得了新的进展和成效。同时，随着国际和区域内各国形势的发展变化，澜湄合作也面临着一些新的挑战。今后应以《澜沧江-湄公河合作五年行动计划》为纲推动澜湄命运共同体建设，注重区域合作规划与澜湄国家和东盟发展规划的对接，以及与其他相关机制的协调发展，构建区域合作大格局。

关键词： 澜湄合作　进展和趋势　支柱领域　优先领域

---

* 刘稚，云南大学澜沧江-湄公河次区域研究中心主任、研究员。

2016 年 3 月正式启动的澜沧江－湄公河合作是中国与周边国家开展区域次区域合作进展最为迅速和最具成效的机制之一。两年来，在中、老、缅、泰、柬、越六方共同努力推动下，澜湄合作建立了领导人会议、外长会议、高官会议、优先领域联合工作组会议等四个层次机制，初步形成了“高效务实、项目为本、民生优先”的合作模式，以“澜湄效率”和“澜湄速度”引起世人瞩目。在当前逆全球化、贸易保护主义、孤立主义等势力甚嚣尘上的背景下，澜湄合作“风景这边独好”，成为次区域合作和国际流域治理的典范。2018 年 1 月 10 日，澜湄合作机制第二次领导人会议在柬埔寨金边举行，会议发表了《澜沧江－湄公河合作五年行动计划（2018～2022）》，为澜湄合作机制未来 5 年的发展规划了蓝图，勾勒出次区域共同繁荣的美好愿景。总体来看，2017 年以来，澜湄合作在取得全面进展的同时，也面临着一些困难和问题，需要我们及时总结，拓展思路，积极推进。

一　澜湄合作的新进展

2017 年以来，澜湄合作机制在政治安全、经济和可持续发展、社会人文三大支柱和互联互通、产能、跨境经济、水资源、农业和减贫五大优先领域的合作都取得了全面进展。同时，澜湄合作机制进一步完善，将“3＋5 合作框架”发展为

“3 +5 +X 合作框架”。6 个成员国在 2017 年都先后成立了澜湄合作国家秘书处或澜湄合作国家协调机构，加强各国跨部门之间的横向联系及成员国之间的协调能力，为推进澜湄合作展开国家层面的协调奠定了基础。同时，还成立了澜湄水资源合作中心、澜湄环境合作中心和全球湄公河研究中心三个辅助性中心，在政策对话、项目合作、人员培训、联合研究等方面提供有力支撑。

（一）三大支柱领域进展平稳

1. 政治安全方面的进展

在政治合作领域，澜湄六国间高层互访频繁、各国间议会、政党、民间团体交流不断。在互访过程中，就双边关系中的问题及共同关注的国际问题进行了战略沟通，强调治国理政经验交流、推动党际交流合作的机制化，促进了相互间的战略互信，为推进澜湄合作提供了政治保障和动力。

在安全领域，2017 年 12 月在昆明正式成立了澜湄次区域第一个综合性执法安全政府间国际组织——澜沧江 - 湄公河综合执法安全合作中心。该中心是中老缅泰湄公河流域执法安全合作的升级版和实体化，将成为次区域国家间预防和打击跨国违法犯罪、情报信息融合交流、专项治理联合行动、加强执法能力建设的综合平台。此外，澜湄国家间在防务、边境安全等方面的合作都在持续推进。

2. 经济和可持续发展

两年来，澜湄合作机制成员国在贸易投资、金融政策协调方面的合作都在持续推进。2017 年中国同五国贸易总额达 2200 亿美元，同比增长 16%。中国累计对五国各类投资超过 420 亿美元，2017 年投资额增长 20% 以上。目前，湄公河国家中除老挝以外，其他国家的第一大贸易伙伴和第一大进口来源国均是中国；而中国则是老挝的第二大贸易伙伴和第三大进口来源国。若将湄公河五国作为一个整体，该地区已是中国的第五大贸易伙伴。与此同时，中国的投资对湄公河国家经济增长越来越重要。从投资存量看，目前中国是柬埔寨、缅甸和老挝最大的外资来源国，越南第四大外资来源国；从投资流量看，2017 年以来中国是泰国第三大外资来源国。

在金融方面，澜湄合作专项基金和中国设立的专项贷款的使用得以推进。截至 2017 年 11 月底，中国设立的第一批专项贷款已完成授信承诺 52.5 亿美元，超额完成 50 亿美元授信评审计划，率先落实首次领导人会议成果，兑现中方对外有关承诺。专项贷款支持了柬埔寨暹粒新机场、老挝万象电力环网、越南永新火电站、泰国开泰银行转贷等 11 个项目，推动澜湄地区电力、交通、产业园区等领域的建设。此外，为了助推贸易和投资便利化，中国和缅甸、柬埔寨加强了金融政策的对接。设在瑞丽市姐告边境贸易区的中缅货币兑换中心运行顺利，促进了中缅跨境投资和贸易结算便利化。

3. 社会人文领域的进展

人文交流是打造“澜湄文化”和“澜湄认同”的重要依托，也是深化澜湄合作的不竭动力。2017 年，澜湄合作框架下的人文交流已经实现了全覆盖，媒体、智库、学者、青年间的往来和交流非常频繁。5 月 22 ~ 29 日，2017 年澜湄大学生友好运动会暨第三届南亚东南亚国家大学生文化体育交流周活动在昆明举办。2017 年 7 月 29 日，首届“澜沧江 - 湄公河青年创新创业训练营”在青海西宁举行，9 月 24 日，澜沧江 - 湄公河文化论坛在浙江宁波举行，澜湄六国文化部长出席，论坛通过了《澜湄文化合作宁波宣言》。

在澜湄合作机制促进下，各国人员往来也日益频繁。自首次领导人会议以来，中国与五国新增航线 330 多条，2017 年人员往来约 3000 万人次。

（二）五大优先领域的进展

2017 年，澜湄机制在互联互通、产能、跨境经济、水资源、农业和减贫五大优先领域的合作在联合工作组的推进下继续取得新的进展。

1. 互联互通领域的进展

2017 年 6 月 13 日在昆明举办了澜湄国家互联互通联合工作组第二次会议，就如何在澜湄合作框架下推进互联互通建设达成了共识。具体进展方面截至 2017 年 10 月末，中老铁路已经全线开工，中泰铁路的建设取得了突破性进展。12 月 21 日，中泰铁路合作项目一期工程开工仪式在呵叻府巴冲县举行。此外，中缅原油管道也于 2017 年 4 月开始正式运营，成为中缅在“一带一路”框架下合作的标志性工程。

2. 产能合作的进展

2017 年 9 月 14 日澜沧江－湄公河国家产能合作联合工作组在广西举行了第二次会议。重点讨论了工作组《概念文件》和下一步工作规划。在具体进展方面，2017 年 2 月 19 日，中国电力建设集团有限公司承建的越南中宋水电站首台机组正式投产发电。由中国南方电网工资投资建设的越南永新燃煤电厂进展顺利，并已经于 2018 年 4 月 18 日成功并网进入运营期。2018 年 1 月 25 日，中国公司承建的老挝川圹省南俄 4 水电站正式开工，将助力老挝“东南亚蓄电池”发展战略的推进。

3. 跨境经济和水资源合作

2017 年 7 月 26 日，澜湄合作跨境经济合作联合工作组第一次会议在云南昆明举行，澜湄国家六方代表签署了《会议纪要》和工作组《职责范围》。2017 年 11 月，习近平主席访问越南时中越两国签署了《加快推进中越跨境经济合作区建设框架协议谈判进程的谅解备忘录》，中缅、中老经济走廊建设也取得重要进展，成为澜湄合作的标志性项目。

2017 年 2 月 27 日，澜湄水资源合作联合工作组第一次会议在北京举行，会议通过了《澜湄水资源合作联合工作组概念文件》和《2017年澜湄水资源合作工作计划》。

4. 农业和减贫合作领域的进展

2017年9月11日。澜湄合作农业联合工作组第一次会议在广西南宁举行，标志着澜湄合作农业联合工作组正式成立。会议就工作组概念文件及下步合作规划等交流了意见，并通过了会议纪要。中国农业部根据湄公河5国的农业需求重点推动实施了四个早期收获项目，内容涉及渔业、水稻、果蔬、豆类等。2017年，中国农业部又成功申请了1378万元澜湄合作专项基金，用于支持实施农业合作项目。在实际行动方面，中国商务部和国务院扶贫办牵头已经在缅甸、老挝和柬埔寨的6个村开展减贫示范合作项目。

二 澜湄合作的发展趋势

1. 早期收获项目示范效应逐步显现

澜湄合作第一次领导人会议确定的45个早期收获项目覆盖五大优先领域，包括水资源管理、生态和环境保护、减贫、防灾、疾病防治、风险评估、旅游及能力建设各个方面。所有项目均为开放的多边合作项目，目前各个早期收获项目全部按计划推进，其中大多数已完成或取得实质性进展。中方在第二次外长会议上又提出13项倡议，也得到各方响应和快速落实。此后，又陆续形成和实施了百余个新的合作项目，释放良好的示范效应，带动了次区域其他项目的落实。

2. 合作的制度性、规划性不断加强

两年来，在六方共同协商和共同努力下，澜湄合作已从成立之初设立的“3+5”合作框架拓展为“3+5+X”合作框架。相关各国均建立了澜湄合作秘书处或协调机构，增进了各国跨部门之间的联系及成员国之间的协调能力，形成“领导人引领、全方位覆盖、各部门参与”的澜湄合作格局。与此同时，六国齐心协力，经过工作组层面的反复磋商、高官会议的研讨、外长会议的定稿，共同编制了第一个《澜湄合作五年行动计划》。这一纲领性文件从区域整体发展角度制定发展规划，在合作机制的基本原则、机制架构、务实合作、支撑体系等方面确立了明确的行为准则，该计划的出台标志着澜湄合作已从探索阶段发展到较为成熟的“规划合作”阶段。

3. 贸易保护主义来袭，倒逼澜湄国家携手共同应对

从国际大环境来看，近年来以美国为代表的单边主义，贸易保护主义兴起，倒逼澜湄次区域各国携手共同应对。中国作为世界上最大的多边新兴市场首当其冲，美国特朗普政府挑起的中美贸易战已将中国逼上了维护自由贸易、多边主义体制的最前线。对此，中国将坚定不移地实行更加开放的政策，大力拓展多元化贸易市场，分散国际贸易风险。湄公河国家尚处在经济发展起飞阶段，市场有限，外向型经济特点突出，且在全球生产网络中处于低端位置，最先感受到逆全球化的冲击，迫切需要加强区域和次区域合作，利用相互之间山水相连、文化相通的地缘人文优势，抱团取暖，通过深化合作来推动域内生产要素快速、高效流动，释放经济活力，共同提升在全球价值链中的地位，推动贸易和投资制度化进程，为区域经济可持续增长注入强劲动力。

4. 成员国经济相互依赖加深，促进区域合作升级

澜湄合作是中国与湄公河五国共同建立的跨国经济区，旨在利用彼此之间生产要素禀赋的不同、通过发挥各方自身比较优势来促进贸易和投资，实现产业综合竞争力提高，提升合作水平。经过长期的经济合作，一方面，中国与湄公河国家经济的相互依赖性、互补性进一步加深，中国已成为湄公河国家最重要的经贸合作伙伴；另一方面，2015 年 1 月中国 - 东盟自由贸易区在越南、缅甸、老挝和柬埔寨等国实现“零关税”，随着削减关税的边际效应降低，拓展合作空间成为日益突出的问题，也驱动了区域合作的升级。

三　深化澜湄合作的路径与对策思考

1. 进一步完善体制机制建设

目前澜湄合作尚处于机制初创阶段，新机制在建立之初动力往往比较强劲，但要保持持久力和活力，则需进一步解决机制赋权问题。世界各国各地区次区域经济合作的经验表明，各国让渡权力的程度，决定着次区域组织的合作深度和广度。今后，澜湄合作要深入推进，需要各国共同寻找利益最大公约数，让渡部分权利给共同的合作体。未来各国需要在加强澜湄合作内部能力建设的基础上，整合各国秘书处或协调机构，搭建统一的执行机构，建立国际秘书处，将澜湄流域作为一个整体进行治理规划，根据各国授权制定保障次区域合作的法律法规。同时，澜湄合作需要不断自我完善，通过制定相关决议、法律文件等形式把合作目标、程序、成果等固化下来，通过合作不断扩大自身影响力。

2. 以《五年行动计划》为纲推动澜湄命运共同体建设

在 2018 年举行的澜湄合作机制第二次领导人会议上，与会各国一致同意并发布了《澜沧江—湄公河合作五年行动计划（2018～2022）》，该行动计划是澜湄合作机制未来五年发展的总纲和指导性文件，并制定了各成员国向外长会提交年度计划落实进展报告的工作架构。根据该行动计划，2018～2019 年是澜湄合作的基础奠定阶段，这期间各国将加强各领域的合作规划、推动中小型合作项目的落地；2020～2022 年为巩固和深化推广阶段，各国将加强五大优先领域合作，逐步开展大项目的合作，并拓展新的合作领域。在此进程中，中国应该发挥引领性作用，与湄公河五国一起逐步落实该行动计划，推动澜湄合作向更深、更宽领域发展，助力澜湄命运共同体建设。

3. 注重区域合作规划与澜湄国家和东盟发展规划的对接

近年来，澜湄各国相继出台本国的发展战略规划。泰国于2016年通过《东部经济特区法》，旨在将泰国东部经济走廊建成泰国深化改革、扩大开放的区域平台；缅甸的《国家全面发展20年规划》重点建设迪拉瓦经济特区——妙瓦底边境口岸经济走廊和皎漂经济特区——木姐边境口岸经济走廊。老挝通过了《2030年愿景规划》和《第八个五年社会经济发展计划》，旨在促进从“陆锁国到陆联国”的变迁。柬埔寨的《四角发展战略》致力于促进经济增长，越南则正在实施《2016～2020年经济社会发展五年规划》，推进国际经济一体化战略。此外，东盟还制定了《东盟互联互通总体规划2025》，促进成员国之间的交通基础设施建设。澜湄合作规划只有基于合作共赢与相关各国及东盟的发展规划对接，形成共同利益来提高各方参与合作的积极性，才能事半功倍，发挥最大效益。

4. 关注下游国家迫切希望获得突破的领域，在水资源合作方面发力

水资源合作是湄公河下游国家最迫切希望获得优先突破的领域。澜湄次区域是中国“一带一路”倡议、“命运共同体”理念最有可能尽快取得成果的方向，因此中国在推进澜湄合作机制的过程中，要充分关注下游国家的核心关切，勇于承担“成长的代价”，全面推进与湄公河五国在水资源方面的合作。制订“水资源合作五年行动计划”，加强旱涝灾害应急管理，开展水资源和气候变化影响等联合研究，按照可持续发展理念，加强水利设施建设等产能合作。根据湄公河国家需求，发挥中国技术装备优势，在湄公河国家参与建设一批水电站、水库、灌溉、饮水工程，实现合作共赢。

5. 注重与其他机制的协调发展，构建区域合作大格局

澜湄合作是一种开放性和包容性的合作，应通过与大湄公河次区域合作、湄委会等构建伙伴关系，有效协调彼此之间的关系，使决策和行动更加合理和科学。今后在条件成熟时，视情可吸收更多的域外国家和国际组织为观察员，协调域内外国家和区域组织之间的关系，促进内部建设与对外扩容并进，适时扩大澜湄合作组织规模，为澜湄合作注入新动力。

要借助五年行动计划优化区域发展格局，将澜湄合作与中国－中南半岛经济走廊、孟中印缅经济走廊、中国－东盟合作机制等相结合，通过澜湄合作与南亚东南亚重要发展规划与战略相衔接，实现澜湄合作效益最大化。在这一进程中，中国作为澜湄合作的主要倡导国，应承担为次区域提供“公共产品”的责任，加强对澜湄合作的政策支持与引领，推动澜湄合作向更高水平迈进。

6. 推进 RCEP 早日生效

在当前全球贸易面临单边主义、保护主义立场挑战的背景下，澜湄六国应与亚洲国家一道积极加快《区域全面经济伙伴关系协定》（RCEP）谈判达成共识，并争取早日生效。尽管 RCEP 成员国之间对开放市场的速度、开放的主要内容、涵盖哪些领域等还有一些分歧，但面对美国加大贸易保护的态度，各方已加快 RCEP 谈判进程并取得积极进展，中方将一如既往地尊重并支持东盟的核心地位和建设性的作用，推动尽早达成一个现代、全面、高质量、互惠的协定，在这一进程中，澜湄合作应发挥重要的促进作用。

澜湄国家地处 RCEP 覆盖范围内，RCEP 的相对高标准规则将会对澜湄合作框架下的贸易和投资便利化产生积极推动作用。具体来说，澜湄六国推进 RCEP 早日生效可从以下几个方面着手。一是加强高层沟通，通过各层次对话平台推动谈判进程，争取率先在若干领域进行政策突破；二是对部分产业设置过渡期和产业损害预警，降低区域内落后国家的参与成本；三是在重大问题上加强磋商，尤其是关于建立多渠道和全方位的争端解决机制，提供贸易和投资救济制度保障。

“一带一路”倡议与东南亚

余　虹*

摘　要： 东南亚地区是中国周边外交政策的优先方向，是推进“一带一路”倡议尤其是海上丝绸之路的核心区域。中国已然成为东南亚国家最重要的合作伙伴之一。中国与东盟的合作具有广度、深度和力度。中国－东盟之间的合作既包括国家层面的双边合作，也涉及包括不同国家在内的多边次区域合作。尤其是在基础设施发展领域，许多东南亚国家在这一领域的国际竞争力排名相当落后，面临本国基础设施老化和严重不足的困扰。中国企业通过布局海外经营与投资，成为东南亚完善基础设施的重要参与者。

关键词： 基础设施　对外投资　中国与东南亚　“一带一路”

---

* 余虹，博士，新加坡国立大学东南亚研究所，高级研究员。

一　东南亚看“一带一路”倡议与中国外交政策转变

过去五年中国通过推进实施“一带一路”倡议，拓展与丝绸之路沿线国家以提升基础设施“互联互通”为导向的投资、贸易和人文交流等领域的合作，深化中国与相关国家的联系。依据2017年11月发布的《中国对外投资报告》①，中国公司成为全球海外直接投资版图中越来越具有分量的参与者：中国在全球海外投资总金额的比重由2002年的0.5%上升到2016年的13.5%。

中国已经成为地区乃至全球基础设施建设领域的领军者，中国在基础设施硬件建设和软件运营管理方面拥有非常强大的实力和完善经验。中国巧妙将以高铁、桥梁和港口为核心的基建设施作为整合区域经济增长的杠杆和加速地区经济一体化的融合剂。“一带一路”正在构建中国与世界互动的新模式，一方面中国在走向世界，另一方面世界也在走向中国。

中国在基础设施建设、装备制造、冶金建材、通信设备

① Ministry of Commerce, People's Republic of China, “*Report on Development of China's Outbound Investment and Economic Cooperation* 2017”（中国对外投资合作发展报告2017），http://fec.mofcom.gov.cn/article/tzhzcj/tzhz/upload/zgdwtzhzfzbg2017.pdf。

等工业领域具有很强的国际竞争力。东南亚很多国家正在加速推进当地工业化和改善基础设施条件，对于引进相关投资、产能和技术有迫切的需求。不少东南亚地区国家将各自国家的发展战略与中国提出的“一带一路”倡议相对接，寻求中国发展带来的机遇和吸引更多中国投资，包括印度尼西亚“全球海洋支点”发展战略、马来西亚“经济转型计划”、柬埔寨“四角战略”、越南“两廊一圈”发展战略以及老挝“陆联国”发展规划。

二　东南亚在“一带一路”倡议中的角色和地位

东南亚地区是中国周边外交政策的优先方向，推进“一带一路”倡议尤其是海上丝绸之路的核心区域。一方面，对于实现中国国家利益而言，东南亚在中国对外关系中的重要性日益显著。东南亚国家参与“一带一路”倡议下的合作深度是检验中国这一倡议能否顺利推进实施乃至取得成功的试金石。中国与东南亚加强经济一体化是双方应对西方贸易保护主义抬头的有效方式，并且有助于减弱外部不稳定因素带给各自经济发展的负面影响。另一方面，自美国总统特朗普主政白宫以来，面对当前美国全球领导力的收缩和西方贸易保护主义日趋显著的趋势，地区国家愿意看到一个更加主动承担更多国际责任的中国出现。

中国已然成为东南亚国家最重要的合作伙伴。中国与东盟的合作具有广度、深度和力度。中国－东盟之间的合作既包括国家层面的双边合作，也涉及包括不同国家在内的多边次区域合作。澜沧江－湄公河流域、泛北部湾合作机制以及正在规划建设的中新陆海贸易新通道都是中国与东盟合作框架下重要的次区域合作平台。2018 年是中国与东盟建立战略伙伴关系 15 周年。中国国务院总理李克强于 2018 年 5 月 7 日到访位于印度尼西亚雅加达的东盟秘书处，展示了中国希望进一步加强与东南亚国家联系和进一步深化双边合作的强烈愿望。

依据中国商务部提供的数据，自 2010 年中国－东盟自由贸易区实施以来，2017 年双边贸易额达到 5148 亿美元，中国已经连续多年成为东盟最大的贸易伙伴和重要的外来投资国。双边人员年度交流往来已经突破 4900 万人次，中国也是东盟国家最大的海外游客来源国。得益于中国与东南亚国家之间程度较高的签证便利化水平，中国公民出境旅游最热门的十大国家主要集中在东南亚。东盟是一个拥有 6 亿多人口和整体经济规模位居世界前列的新兴经济体。东盟地区资源丰富和市场潜力巨大，经济稳步成长，中产阶级人口不断增长，劳动力人口相对年轻，吸引了越来越多国际投资者的目光。①

① 余虹：《“一带一路”、中国崛起与国际合作》，世界知识出版社，2017。

三 "一带一路"倡议下中国对东南亚投资

世界经济论坛2017年公布的全球基建设施竞争力指标排名[①]显示：许多东南亚国家在这一领域的竞争力排名相当落后，面临本国基础设施老化和严重不足的困扰。根据亚洲开发银行在2017年发布的一份研究报告[②]，为了实现年度平均5%以上经济增长目标和应对气候变化带来的挑战，从2016年到2030年，仅东南亚国家就需要总计3.14万亿美元的基础设施投资额。传统经济地理理论发现高效而便捷的现代交通基础设施是实现国家经济起飞和工业化的前提和关键所在。[③] 但是，许多东南亚国家面临建设现代基础设施的艰巨任务，尤其是菲

① World Economic Forum, "The Global Competitiveness Report 2017 - 2018," Geneva, pp. 1 - 380.

② 亚洲开发银行，"满足亚洲基础设施建设需求"，2017年2月，https://www.adb.org/zh/news/asia-infrastructure-needs-exceed-17-trillion-year-double-previous-estimates。

③ P. Krugman, Geography and Trade, Cambridge: MIT Press, 1991; P. Krugman, "The Role of Geography in Development," *International Regional Science Review*, 22: 2, pp. 142 - 161; S. Brakman, H. Garretsen, and C. V. Marrewijk, *An Introduction to Geographical Economics: Trade, location and growth*, Cambridge: Cambridge University Press, 2001; S. Redding and A. J. Venables, "Economic Geography and International Inequality", CEPR mimeo, April 2001, London; Yu Hong, *Economic Development and Inequality in China*, London and New York: Routledge, 2011.

律宾、老挝、柬埔寨和缅甸。基础设施的落后与运输能力不足阻碍这些国家实现经济快速增长。由于这些国家经济发展落后，它们缺乏独立完成庞大基建工程所需的资金和技术能力。中国主导下的“一带一路”倡议①与“东盟地区共同体愿景2025”和“东盟互联互通总体规划2025”② 有共通之处，都旨在通过改善基础设施条件，促进区域之间的互联互通。在“一带一路”合作框架下，中国愿意支持东盟共同体建设，也有能力通过增加融资来支持东盟地区互联互通进程。

中国企业通过大规模布局海外经营与投资，成为东南亚完善基础设施的重要参与者。中国对“一带一路”沿线国家投资存量排名前十的国家中，东南亚地区国家占到6个，包括新加坡、印度尼西亚、老挝、越南、缅甸和泰国。尤其是2017年，新加坡超越美国，成为中国企业海外并购的第一大目的地。基于其作为亚洲重要的金融中心和航运中心的地位，新加坡是中国企业对外投资主要目的地之一。新加坡在中国推进“一带一路”倡议中占有特殊重要地位。

① Ministry of Foreign Affairs, People's Republic of China, "*Vision and Actions on Jointly Building Silk Road Economic Belt and 21st Century Maritime Silk Road* ", http: //www. fmprc. gov. cn/mfa _ eng/zxxx _ 662805/t1249618. shtml.

② The ASEAN Secretariat, "Master Plan on ASEAN Connectivity 2025," Jakarta, 2016, pp. 1 – 115, http: //asean. org/storage/2016/09/Master – Plan – on – ASEAN – Connectivity – 20251. pdf.

小结

中国外交政策的发展和推进实施“一带一路”倡议不仅将给中国带来深远的影响，也将在很大程度上重新定义中国与世界的联系和互动模式。中国推进“一带一路”倡议也将给亚洲乃至全球地缘政治和经济格局带来深远的影响。尽管包括东南亚在内一些周边国家对中国崛起抱有戒心，还没有完全适应中国崛起带来的区域形势变化，但总的趋势是积极的。

“一带一路”倡议需要中国赢得区域国家的信任，需要取得丝绸之路沿线国家对该倡议的支持。对于像“一带一路”这样的宏大倡议而言，中国无力也无法独自推动该倡议，“一带一路”倡议最终要取得成功需要寻求国际社会的合作，需要丝路沿线地区和国家的共同参与。

人类命运共同体与
中国－东盟命运共同体

从率先倡议到优先实践

——周边命运共同体构建的理论与实践

石源华*

摘　要： 命运共同体的率先倡议始于中国周边地区，继而扩展至整个亚洲和全球。本文从周边命运共同体构建的视角，论述其理论和实践的基本内涵和现实意义，阐述命运共同体构建表达了中国与周边国家和平相处的“共生哲学”，体现了中国走向大国时代的“历史使命”，形成了中国对美国强势制衡的“太极应对”，构筑了中国与周边共谋发展繁荣的“系统工程”，建树了中国与周边关系走向未来的理论体系。周边国家和周边地区是人类命运共同体倡议建设的始发之地、重点之地、关键之地、示范之地，也是决定兴衰成败之地。

---

* 石源华，复旦大学国际问题研究院中国与周边国家关系研究中心主任，教授。

关键词： 周边命运共同体　率先倡议　优先实践

一　从率先倡议到优先实践

周边地区是习近平倡导命运共同体构建的关键地区。“命运共同体”的提法最早出现于2011年国务院新闻办公室发布的《中国的和平发展》白皮书。[①] 2012年，中共十八大报告正式写入了建立“人类命运共同体”的新概念。习近平执政后，更加重视和强调命运共同体建设，将其提升为中国走向强国大国时代的最重要的理论旗帜和战略目标。

命运共同体的率先倡议始于中国周边地区。2013年3月，习近平首访俄罗斯，在莫斯科国际关系学院发表演讲，强调在全球化背景下国家之间“应成为你中有我、我中有你的命运共同体”[②]。为此，两国签署联合声明，开启了中俄命运共同体的建设历程。[③] 随后，中国与众多周边国家签署了建设各种形式的命运共同体协议。2013年10月3日，习近平在印度尼

① 国务院新闻办公室：《中国的和平发展》白皮书，《新华每日电讯》2011年9月6日。

② 习近平：《顺应时代前进潮流　促进世界和平发展——在莫斯科国际关系学院演讲》，《人民日报》2013年3月23日。

③ 《中华人民共和国与俄罗斯联邦关于合作共赢、深化全面战略协作伙伴关系的联合声明》，《人民日报》2013年3月23日。

西亚国会发表“携手建设中国－东盟命运共同体”的演讲，提议以讲信修睦、合作共赢、守望相助、心心相印、开放包容五大举措，建设“中国－东盟命运共同体”。[①] 2015 年 4 月 6 日，中国在北京举办“六个国家，一个命运共同体”的澜湄对话合作高官会，首创打造周边命运共同体的澜湄次区域合作机制。[②] 命运共同体建设倡议从单个国家扩展至周边的东盟和澜湄次区域地区。

命运共同体的构建倡议和实践继而扩展至整个亚洲和全球。2015 年 3 月 28 日，习近平在博鳌论坛年会发表《迈向命运共同体　开创亚洲新未来》演讲，提出建设“亚洲命运共同体”倡议。[③] 9 月 28 日，习近平在美国纽约联合国第 70 届大会上发表《携手构建合作共赢新伙伴，同心打造人类命运共同体》，将命运共同体建设推向联合国。[④] 2017 年 1 月 18 日，习近平在联合国日内瓦总部发表《共同构建人类命运共同体》，全面阐述中国建设人类命运共同体的主张和目标。[⑤]

---

① 石源华主编《中国周边外交研究报告（2015～2016）》，世界知识出版社，2106，第 221 页。

② 石源华主编《中国周边外交研究报告（2015～2016）》，世界知识出版社，2106，第 221 页。

③ 习近平：《迈向命运共同体开创亚洲新未来》，《人民日报》2015 年 3 月 29 日。

④ 习近平：《习近平谈治国理政》第二卷，外文出版社，2017，第 521～526 页。

⑤ 习近平：《谈治国理政》第二卷，第 537～549 页。

建设“人类命运共同体”很快写入联合国决议，成为联合国实现全球治理的重要纲领性主张，成为中国治理全球主张的目标和旗帜。

2017 年 11 月 30 日～12 月 3 日，中共中央以“构建人类命运共同体，共同建设美好世界：政党的责任”为主题举行世界政党高层对话会，规模宏大，习近平发表主旨讲话，对人类命运共同体内涵以及构建思路做了进一步的阐述，提出：“在新型国际关系的基础上，建立求同存异、相互尊重、互学互鉴的新型政党关系，汇聚构建人类命运共同体的强大力量。”① 从优先实践的重要角度，阐述在世界范围构建人类命运共同体的理念。

由此可见，习近平和中国共产党对于“命运共同体”阐述和践行始于中国周边国家和周边地区，从命运共同体协议、“中国与东盟命运共同体”、“澜湄六国命运共同体”、“亚洲命运共同体”开始，进而推向“亚太命运共同体”“人类命运共同体”等，经历了由周边国家、周边地区、泛周边地区（亚太、印太），最终走向全球（联合国）的发展路径，逐步将“命运共同体”建设扩展成为联合国确认的全人类共同的努力方向和奋斗目标。人类命运共同体理念得到国际社会越来越多

① 郑长忠：《推动构建人类命运共同理念下的新型政党关系》，《当代世界》2018 年第 1 期。

的认同和支持，中国理念逐步得到国际认同，中国倡议日益成为全球行动。中国的议题设置和话语构建能力持续增强。[①]

周边国家和周边地区是人类命运共同体倡议和建设的始发之地、重点之地、关键之地、示范之地，也是决定兴衰成败之地。本文将从周边命运共同体构建的视角，论述其理论和实践的基本内涵和现实意义。

二 中国与周边和平相处的“共生哲学”

命运共同体构建体现了中国与周边国家和平相处的“共生哲学”。中国周边亚洲的复杂性超过任何一个大洲。亚洲同时拥有几大宗教，不同地区人们的价值观念有很大的差异，各国之间领土、领海纠纷众多，经济发展水平差距很大，政治制度各不相同。对于中国来说，来自周边地区的牵制和阻挠呈现增多之势，既有周边国家“内乱”或次区域冲突涉及中国，也有中外领土、领海争端，成为美国推行制衡中国战略的借口和抓手，给实现中华民族伟大复兴中国梦带来重大障碍。中国崛起能否成功，在很大程度上取决于中国能否善于与周边国家

① 季思：《人类命运共同体理念彰显中国共产党国际话语的历史穿透力》，《当代世界》2018 年第 3 期。

和平共处，分享发展机会，拓展合作共赢的空间。[①]

习近平在莫斯科国际关系学院演讲中阐述了我们所处时代的新特点：其一是“和平、发展、合作、共赢成为时代潮流。旧殖民体系土崩瓦解，冷战时期的集团对抗不复存在，任何国家和国家集团都再也无法单独主宰世界”。其二是“一大批新兴市场国家和发展中国家走上发展的快车道，十几亿、几十亿人口正在加速走向现代化，多个发展中心在世界各地区逐渐形成，国际力量对比继续朝着有利于世界和平与发展的方向发展”。其三是“各国相互联系、相互依存的程度空前加深，人类生活在同一个地球村里，生活在历史和现实的同一时空里，越来越成为你中有我、我中有你的命运共同体”。其四是“人类依然面临诸多难题和挑战，国际金融危机深层次影响继续显现，形形色色的保护主义明显升温，地区热点此起彼伏，霸权主义、强权政治和新干涉主义有所上升，军备竞争、恐怖主义、网络安全等传统安全威胁和非传统安全威胁相互交织，维护世界和平、促进共同发展依然任重道远”。[②] 习近平不仅明确提出“命运共同体”的新概念，作为应对新时代的治世之方，而且指出“不能身体已进入21世纪，而脑袋还停留在过

① 石源华：《中共十八大中国周边外交研究报告》，社会科学文献出版社，2016，第30～31页。

② 习近平：《顺应时代前进潮流　促进世界和平发展——在莫斯科国际关系学院演讲》，《人民日报》2013年3月23日。

去，停留在殖民扩张和旧时代里，停留在冷战思维、零和博弈的老框框内”。[①]

在此基础上，习近平提出了中国与周边国家和平相处的“共生哲学”以取代那些过时的以弱肉强食、霸权稳定论为主要特征的“治世法则”，并对此做了深刻而完整的理论阐述和政策概括，主要包括四个要点。

第一，“坚持各国相互尊重、平等相待”，主张“涉及大家的事情需要同各国商量来办”，“要尊重各国自主选择的社会制度和发展道路，客观理性等看待别国发展壮大和政策理念，尊重彼此核心利益和重大关切，努力求同存异、聚同化异”，“反对干涉别国内政，反对为一己私利搞乱地区形势”。

第二，“坚持合作共赢，共同发展”，主张“只有合作共赢才能办大事，办好事，办长久之事”，强调“摒弃零和游戏、你输我赢的旧思维，树立双赢、共赢的新理念，在追求自身利益时兼顾他方利益，在寻求自身发展时促进共同发展”。

第三，“坚持实现共同、综合、合作、可持续的安全”，认为“当今世界，没有一个国家能实现世界不安全的自身安全”，强调“摒弃冷战思维，创新安全理论，努力走出一条共建、共享、共赢的亚洲之路”。

① 习近平：《顺应时代前进潮流　促进世界和平发展——在莫斯科国际关系学院演讲》，《人民日报》2013 年 3 月 23 日。

第四，“坚持不同文明兼容，交流互览”，强调“要促进不同文明、不同发展模式交流对话，在竞争比较中取长补短，在交流互鉴中取长补短，让文明交流互鉴成为增进各国人民友谊的桥梁、推动人类社会进步的动力、维护世界和平的纽带”。①

中国积极推进命运共同体成为中国与周边区域各国的“共生哲学”和大多数国家的共识，中国搭建了越来越多的合作共赢平台，为各国汇聚共同利益提供更多的支点，取得了良好效果。泰国前副总理素拉杰对此高度评价说：“亚洲命运共同体不仅仅是逐步形成的概念，更是一种哲学。它提醒我们亚洲人，我们曾经是多么分裂，被各种战争、各种制度、各种分歧所分裂；而今天，命运共同体这个具有哲学高度的概念引起了亚洲人的共鸣”，“亚洲应该迈向一个新未来，忘却历史恩怨、追求和平发展的未来。”②

三　中国走向大国时代的“历史使命”

人类命运共同体提出和推行的时代，正是中国从富起来走

① 习近平：《迈向命运共同体，开创亚洲新未来》，《人民日报》2015年3月29日。

② 《泰国前副总理素拉杰：让“一带一路”沿线国跟上中国节奏》，《参考消息》2015年4月1日。

向强起来的时代。习近平在中共十九大报告中指出："今天，我们比历史上任何时期都更接近、更有信心和能力实现中华民族伟大复兴的目标。"报告清晰擘画了全面建成社会主义现代化强国的时间表和路线图：从现在到2020年，全面建成小康社会，实现第一个"百年"奋斗目标；其后，再奋斗15年，2035年基本实现社会主义现代化；再奋斗15年，2050年实现第二个"百年"奋斗目标，把我国建设成富强民主文明和谐美丽的社会主义现代化强国。① 至少在2035年前中国周边外交仍将居外交全局的首要地位。

在这个阶段，中国处于从富起来到强起来、从发展中国家到发达国家、从将强未强到世界级强国的历史转变进程之中。中国的GDP总量与美国还有较大的差距，2017年，美国的GDP总量是19.36万亿美元，中国是12.24万亿美元，中国虽然稳居第二，与美国之间的距离也正以较快速度在缩小，但仅是美国的63.2%。中国人均GDP则处于世界排名较后的位置。2017年，美国人均GDP为59495美元，中国人均GDP为8582美元，是美国的14.4%，中美间的实力差距非常明显。② 为此，中国最应当关注的是做强做大自身，避免将全球注意力吸

① 《习近平代表第十八届中央委员会向大会作的报告摘要》，《新华每日电讯》2017年10月19日。

② 《2017年世界GDP排名》《2017年世界人均GDP排名》，世界经济信息网，http://www.8pu.com/gdp/ranking_2017.html。

引到自己身上来，继续争取长期稳定发展的机遇，使中国稳步成为一个世界级的强国。中国主要发挥影响力的地区仍是中国周边，中国的历史性任务是引领亚洲，避免发生颠覆性的错误。中国不宜急于为世界性权力心动，不能给世人造成中国急于要取代美国的印象，不宜急于提出和推广以全球事务为对象的“中国方案”，更不宜急于企图以某种新体系主导国际社会。

在这样的背景之下，倡议建设“人类命运共同体”，重点在中国周边地区推行，成为中国步向大国时代的中国外交大战略和周边外交实际运作的最佳方略。命运共同体的历史使命将表现为：它是中国走向大国外交新时代的纲领性理论旗帜，有助于清除“中国威胁论”的鼓噪和喧嚣，树立中国特色社会主义大国的良好形象；它也是中国与美国霸权稳定论和强权政治相比较而提出的全球治理战略，在世人面前形成不同的国际形象，有助于稳定世界形势大局；它也是中国与广大周边国家发展双边关系或多边关系的实际指导方针，有助于以“亲诚惠容”新理念发展及周边国家与区域组织的好邻居、好朋友、好伙伴关系；它更是中国成为世界大国强国后处理对外关系的重要预演，为实现“中国强大后不称霸”诺言给世人做出榜样和示范。

四 中国对美国强势制衡的“太极应对”

建设命运共同体是中国对美国强势制衡中国的“太极应对”之法，卓有成效。冷战结束后，特别是中国成为世界第二大经济体后，中国周边安全格局出现两重性特点：一方面，中国快速崛起和美国霸权守成构成了中国周边的内在结构性矛盾，在一个短时期内难以得到解决，美国对华制衡将成为中国面临的主要安全威胁。另一方面，中美不发生大的对抗是双方底线，中国主导的多边安全体系与美国主导的双边同盟体系，在中国周边实现“兼容共存”，导致中美内在结构性矛盾不体现对抗性特点。[①]

特朗普上任，将其强烈的民粹主义取向与“美国优先”理念带入美国的内政外交之中，他张扬率性、口无遮拦的个性和“逢奥巴马必反”的执政风格，引发第二次世界大战以来美国对外关系大变局。朝鲜半岛问题、钓鱼岛问题、台海问题、南海问题、贸易战问题等，处处显现中美结构性矛盾依然尖锐存在，特朗普视中国为主要竞争对手的“零和”思维与历届美国总统无异，美国对华遏制和制衡已成双边关系主流，

① 石源华：《三议特朗普时代的东亚政治安全格局》，《世界知识》2017年第15期。

中国周边成为中美较量的前沿阵地和主要地区。

面对美国汹涌而来的强势制衡，中国淡定、沉着、冷静判断美国是阻碍中国崛起和破坏中国周边安全平衡的主要国家，不对其抱不切实际的幻想，但不采取正面对抗之策，不走新兴大国与守成大国通过对抗实现更迭的老路，不重犯苏联与美国在冷战期间正面军备争霸招致失败的教训，坚持继续在既成国际体系和规则下实现强国目标。

对于美国的强势制衡，是你做你的“军事威胁”“联盟制衡”“贸易恶战”“颜色革命”，我做我的“命运共同体”“一带一路”“合作共赢”“亚洲安全观”，表现出“太极应对”式的柔性抗争特点。你在我近海频频搅局，我则冲破第一岛链，巡航南太平洋，进入印度洋，甚至与俄罗斯联合在日本海、西太平洋和北约门户地中海进行军演，展示中国的存在和海军的进步。你在中国东部海上挑起各种事端，制造紧张空气，围堵压迫中国，我则另辟蹊径，向西部发展，在广袤的、长期不稳定的欧亚大陆，倡议建设“丝绸之路经济带”，实现互联互通，合作共赢，开辟新的战略方向，进而在中国周边实现全方位合作和互利共赢。① 你张牙舞爪，气势汹汹，向中国发起贸易战，我在以牙还牙强硬反击的同时，将开放的大门越

① 石源华：《“一带一路”与中国周边合作全覆盖》，复旦大学中国与周边国家关系研究中心编《中国周边外交学刊》2015 年第 2 辑，第 43 页。

开越大，以“开放与创新”作为对美不战而胜的战略大政。[①] 中国所采取的“命运共同体”“一带一路”“合作共赢”“亚洲安全观”“开放与创新”，成功抗衡美国的强势制衡中国之举，既维护了中国周边的和平与安全，使美国这样信奉霸权主义，惯于实行炮舰政策，有着熟练外交技能的国家，无计可施，又能避免中美间的激烈冲突，以有理、有利、有节的坚决斗争，迫使美国从“冷战化危险”中走出。双方重视和尊重各自在中国周边的重大战略关切和核心利益，从而控制了中美内在结构性矛盾的扩张，扩大了“兼容共存”和合作共赢的空间，维持中国周边安全平衡，有利于两个大国的长远利益。

五　中国与周边共谋发展繁荣的“系统工程”

建设命运共同体也是中国与周边国家发展友好关系、实现共同发展繁荣的“系统工程”。笔者以为在中国周边已经出现了新的“三个世界”架构：中美各为一极，其间存在许多“中间国家”。这些国家中虽然一度出现日本、越南、菲律宾、新加坡、韩国、印度等国不同程度地利用美国推行“亚太再平衡”战略谋取私利的各种举动，损害甚至侵犯中国的国家

① 习近平：《中国开放的大门只会越开越大》（2018 年 4 月 10 日），《人民日报》2018 年 4 月 11 日。

利益，但这些国家的自身国家利益决定其基本立场终将仍是在中美之间寻求“平衡”，一般不会或不会永远在中美之间做“非此即彼”的选择，这与冷战时代有重要区别。①

争取更多的中间国家站在自己一边，或更多地倾向自己，成为中美两国博弈的重要内容。从克林顿、小布什、奥巴马到特朗普，美国历届政府都一以贯之，推行分化、挑拨、撕裂中国与周边国家关系的政策，如利用中日钓鱼岛争端等分裂中日关系，利用“萨德入韩”将处于发展高峰期的中韩关系颠覆谷底，利用南海争端分裂中国与菲律宾和越南的关系，利用朝核问题力图使美朝对抗转化为中朝分歧甚至对抗，中印洞朗对峙也有美国挑唆的背景等。为此，中国有必要从战略层面关注和研讨如何深化与中国周边“中间国家”密切关系问题，建设中国与周边国家长远友好关系的“系统工程”。

建设命运共同体，实现中国与周边国家的合作共赢，可以破除和瓦解美国等域外大国对于中国和周边国家的分化和分裂政策，按照“亲诚惠容”理念和“以邻为善、以邻为伴”周边外交方针，深化与所有周边国家的友好关系，使它们更多地不仅在经济上也在安全上与中国实现合作共赢。

建设命运共同体，按照“双轨思路”解决中国与周边国

① 本节参见石源华《中国周边已经出现新的“三个世界”架构》的主要观点，《世界知识》2017 年第 15 期。

家间的分歧和争端，可以清除域外大国的挑拨和干扰，避免引发互相间的冲突和激化，寻找到妥善解决的和平之道，从而实现地区的合作稳定，合作共赢。

建设命运共同体，可充分发挥中国在周边国家发展中的核心力量和中流砥柱作用，通过“一带一路”建设，与周边国家真正实现“五通”，进而为命运共同体在全球范围内推广做出榜样与示范。

建设命运共同体，还应理解、接受和正确对待“中间国家”在中美间实行平衡政策。冷战时期那种非此即彼、画线站队式对待中间国家的态度已经过时。中国应以包容的态度争取与所有周边国家建立友好关系，以建设命运共同体为指导和标向，与周边国家建设共同发展繁荣的“系统工程”。

六　中国与周边关系走向未来的理论建树

中共十九大确定的习近平新时代中国特色社会主义思想，既要超越和扬弃东方传统理论体系，总结和吸取其合理内核，创建符合时代需求和民族特点的中国特色新理论，更要打破和超越西方国际关系理论体系，吸收和借鉴其合理成分，摒弃和克服西方国际关系理论已经日益显露的种种弊病，阐述习近平提出的以“合作共赢”为核心理念的中国特色国际关系和大国外交理论新体系。[①] 这个理论新体系将在扬弃、清理西方旧理论体系并与之进行较量和冲突的过程中逐步形成。命运共同体理论是习近平时代中国特色社会主义思想关于国际关系和大国外交理论体系的重要组成部分，具有重要的理论意义和现实意义。

在战略层面，命运共同体将破除西方世界惯行的“势力范围”理论和旧有的“圈地”陋规，树立以“合作共赢”为核心理念的国际关系新范式，阐述中国并非如西方世界指责的那样通过“一带一路”在中国周边建立“势力范围”，亦并非如西方马汉“海权论”所主张的建立“海洋霸权”，而是在“和谐世界”的理念下，在中国周边建设“合作共赢”的“命运共同体”。

在经济层面，命运共同体理论将破除西方主导世界经济的旧地缘政治经济理论和旧全球化范式，总结和阐述“一带一路”倡议是在“共商、共建、共享”的原则下，与中国周边所有的参与者平等合作，为周边国家提供新的发展和合作平台，为周边区域治理提供新的公共产品，并为周边国家全方位的经济合作提供新的方案。

在安全层面，命运共同体理论将破除西方主导世界的

① 参见蒋昌建、潘忠岐《人类命运共同体理论对西方国际关系理念的扬弃》，《浙江学刊》2017 年第 4 期。

“同盟体系论”和“零和博弈论”，在亚洲彻底清除冷战残余，通过总结“一带一路”与周边外交实施的实践，创新安全理念，实施“共同、综合、合作、可持续”的“亚洲安全观”，推动中国周边地区的和平与合作。

在政治层面，命运共同体理论将破除西方主导世界的“霸权稳定论”和强权政治逻辑，通过总结“一带一路”和中国周边合作共赢外交的理论和实践创新，展示该理论与美国倡导的“霸权稳定论”代表世界不同的发展方向和路径，中国将通过与各国共同的和平努力，开创以“命运共同体”为目标的中国与周边国家和平建设的新局面，实现中国强大起来后仍不称霸的庄严承诺。

在理论层面，命运共同体理论将超越和扬弃西方国际关系理论体系，吸收其理论精华，克服其已经日益显露的种种弊病，阐述习近平提出的以“合作共赢”为核心理念、以“命运共同体”为建设目标的国际关系理论新体系和“一带一路”背景下中国特色大国周边外交的新理念、新战略和新路径，推动“一带一路”和中国周边外交更加健康发展。

命运共同体在中国周边的实施将为新时代中国特色社会主义思想关于国际关系和大国外交理论做出重要的理论建树，为中国与周边国家共同和平走向未来确定明确的战略目标。

Singapore – China Relations: Seeking Continued Relevance through Greater Connectivity

Lye Liang Fook *

It has been almost five years since Chinese President Xi Jinping unveiled China's Belt and Road Initiative (BRI) while visiting Kazakhstan in September 2013 and Indonesia in October 2013. Since then, many projects related to BRI have been rolled out in the more than 65 countries that line the BRI with varying degrees of success and achievement.

---

* Lye Liang Fook is a Senior Fellow and Co-Coordinator of the Vietnam Studies Programme at the Institute of Southeast Asian Studies-Yusof Ishak Institute. The views here are entirely his own and do not represent those of the institute.

At a symposium to mark the fifth anniversary of the BRI in Beijing in August 2018, President Xi indicated that China will continue to press ahead with the BRI to transform it into a high quality development initiative（向高质量发展转变）. Using the analogy of a Chinese painting, President Xi said that over the past five years, the BRI, where China has worked in tandem with other countries, has essentially completed its overall layout or has been painted with a broad and free hand（大写意）. Going forward, he said there was a need to meticulously focus on the detailed strokes（工笔画）. This would include paying more attention to the needs of recipient countries by ensuring that BRI projects are able to provide the necessary warmth during snowy weather, render assistance where it is needed most and benefit the local people in terms of projects related to their livelihood（注意实施雪中送炭、急对方之所急、能够让当地老百姓受益的民生工程）.① China's decision to continue with BRI and to accord more attention to the implementation process as well as the benefits that it will bring to the recipient countries are timely and

① "Xi Jinping zai tuijin 'yidai yilu' jianshe gongzuo wu zhounian zuotanhui shang qiangdiao jianchi duihua xieshang gongjian gongxiang hezuo gongying jiaoliu hujian tuidong gongjian 'yidai yilu' zoushen zoushi zaofu renmin", *Xinhua News*, 27 August 2018.

most welcomed. This adjustment can provide a more sustainable basis for countries to collaborate and make further progress with China together.

Singapore has been an early supporter of China's BRI and was among the first batch of 21 countries that signed the MOU to mark the launch of the China-led Asian Infrastructure Investment Bank (AIIB), a multilateral financial institution supporting the building of infrastructural projects in developing countries. At the AIIB's launch in Beijing in October 2014, Singapore's Deputy Prime Minister and Finance Minister Tharman Shanmugaratnam, who represented Singapore at the launch, said that the "AIIB is a positive development which will help to meet the immense infrastructure needs in Asia" and that Singapore "looks forward to working with other members to establish the AIIB as a resilient multilateral institution, complementing and drawing on best practices of existing players like the World Bank and Asian Development Bank, so as to promote sustained growth in Asia".①

① "Deputy Prime Minister and Minister for Finance, Mr. Tharman Shanmugaratnam signs MOU on establishing the Asian Infrastructure Investment Bank", *Singapore's Ministry of Finance press release*, 24 October 2014.

On the Maritime Silk Road (or Road) in particular, Singapore's Prime Minister Lee Hsien Loong was reported to have said in November 2014 that if Singapore can deepen its cooperation with "neighbouring countries, and in particular, strengthen trade and investment between China and its neighbours through the Maritime Silk Road initiative, we hope a part of the services can be provided through Singapore's sea port and airport network". ①In other words, Singapore sees in the Maritime Silk Road fresh opportunities to grow and re-affirm its status as a major transportation, logistics, maritime and financial hub.

Singapore has been equally supportive of the Silk Road Economic Belt (or Belt). During the state visit of Chinese President Xi Jinping to Singapore in November 2015, Singapore and China announced that they would embark on a government-to-government (G-to-G) venture in Chongqing known as the China-Singapore (Chongqing) Demonstrative Initiative on Strategic Connectivity (Chongqing Connectivity Initiative). This initiative fits in with China's strategy to develop its inland areas through the Belt initiative. Since that visit, the two countries have been

① "Singapore can Leverage a Revived Silk Road", *Business Times* (Singapore), 11 November 2014.

working hard to get more businesses to collaborate in the four main areas of transport and logistics, financial services, aviation and ICT.

From Singapore's standpoint, the Maritime Silk Road and Silk Road Economic Belt ought not to operate independently but can develop synergies with and complement one another. It was with this in mind that Singapore proposed the idea of the Chongqing Connectivity Initiative-Southern Transport Corridor in 2017 so that this corridor will link Chongqing, a key node on the Silk Road Economic Belt, via railroad to Qin zhou Port in Guangxi Autonomous Region, and from Qin zhou Port to other parts of Southeast Asia and beyond via sea links. In a way, the corridor provides a strategic link that marries the Belt with the Road. The corridor is a key demonstration of Singapore's effort to stay relevant to China's growth through pursuing greater connectivity with China.

Even way before the Chongqing Connectivity Initiative and Southern Transport Corridor was proposed, Singapore has constantly adopted a proactive approach of pursuing connectivity with China through practical and substantive cooperation. Apart from the Chongqing Connectivity Initiative which is the third G-to-G project between Singapore and China, there are two other G-to-

G projects such as the Suzhou Industrial Park and the Tianjin Eco-city respectively. These three G-to-G projects underscore Singapore's constant effort to explore areas of cooperation with China that meet the needs of the two countries. They also show that the two countries are continuously reviewing the state of their collaboration, to either broaden or deepen existing areas of cooperation or to explore new ones.

This paper will focus on the Chongqing Connectivity Initiative-Southern Transport Corridor by highlighting the objective and key aspects of this initiative. It will also dwell on the significance and challenges faced in promoting this initiative. Before turning to the Chongqing Connectivity Initiative-Southern Transport Corridor, it would be worthwhile to have a brief overview of the two earlier G-to-G projects, namely the Suzhou Industrial Park and the Tianjin Eco-city, in order to better understand how the Chongqing Connectivity Initiative differs from these two earlier projects although they are all related to building connectivity between Singapore and China as well as China and the rest of the world.

Rationale for Each G-to-G Project

(a) Suzhou Industrial Park (SIP)

In 1994, when Jiang Zemin was Chinese president, Singapore and China embarked on a plan to develop a 70-square kilometre (km^2) site with industrial, commercial and residential components on the east side of old Suzhou city in the direction of Shanghai. ① From the start, both sides agreed that the SIP had to be commercially viable for it to be sustainable. In this sense, the SIP was no different from other industrial parks in that the market would be the key determinant of its success.

Yet, the SIP was at the same time different from other industrial parks in that it was driven by the governments of the two countries. This G-to-G component was essential because the SIP involved software transfer from the Singapore side to the Chinese side. The term Singapore software may defy easy description but it is essentially manifested in Singapore's laws, rules, regulations,

① Today, the SIP has a size of 288 km^2 and the original Singapore-China cooperation zone of 70 km^2 has been expanded to 80 km^2.

together with its work processes and systems and, most important of all, in the values and problem-solving attitudes of its experienced officers. Such software has underpinned Singapore's rapid socio-economic progress since independence in 1965. Singapore sought to share its experience by working jointly with China to develop the SIP. Such a practical and hands-on approach over an extended period of time was considered a much more effective way for Singapore to share its development experience compared to the short visits by numerous other Chinese delegations to Singapore.

Some of the distinctive elements that Singapore shared with their Chinese counterparts included the importance of having an overall plan (such as master planning) and long-term planning; providing one-stop service; being responsive to investors' needs and promoting transparency and predictability in the operating environment. These are important in attracting investors to set up shop and to remain in SIP. For residents, the emphasis is on providing easy and convenient access to facilities and amenities, inculcating a sense of community and creating a liveable environment through, for instance, greening efforts and setting aside sufficient green spaces. Today, the concept of neighborhood centres where residents' daily needs andamenities such as supermarkets, restaurants, shopping malls, banks, childcare centres, outpatient clinics and libraries can be found under one roof or at one particular location has become part and parcel of life in SIP.

The above may be standard fare today, but they were quite unfamiliar concepts when proposed in Suzhou in the 1990s. At that time, China was still reeling from the negative fallout of the 1989 Tiananmen incident and the SIP fitted in well with China's objective to jumpstart its economy. The partnership with Singapore with a good international reputation, coupled with elements of Singapore's DNA through its software transfer, was considered a valued proposition to attract international investors. This Singapore element, which has remained to this day, is still considered an attractive feature of the SIP today by the SIP Administrative Committee as it grapples with the constant task of industrial upgrading to find new sources of growth such as in biopharmaceuticals, nanotechnology and cloud computing. Both SIP as well as Singapore are in transition towards high value-added and R&D-intensive industries and both see value in continued collaboration so as to benefit from each other's experiences.

Furthermore, the software transfer that started in 1994 has continued to this day. According to some sources, as of

September 2018, Singapore has trained a total of 3600 Chinese officials under the software training programme. ①In line with the development needs of the SIP, the training focus has shifted to cover areas such as foreign investment and cooperation, international trade and finance, industrial structure upgrading and optimisation, and social governance. Singapore has indicated that it will continue to provide such software transfer as long as the Chinese side sees value in them.

(b) Tianjin Eco-city

Singapore's Senior Minister Goh Chok Tong first mooted this project when he visited Beijing in April 2007 and called on China's Premier Wen Jiabao. A framework agreement was signed in November 2007 to embark on the eco-city project which was followed by a ground-breaking ceremony in September 2008.

The Tianjin Eco-city was in line with the shift in development emphasis by Beijing. In 2003, President Hu Jintao enunciated the Scientific Outlook on Development to tackle mounting problems

---

① In addition, since the mid-1990s and to date, more than 50000 Chinese officials have come to Singapore for various study visits and training programmes. See Singapore's Ministry of Foreign Affairs website at https://www.mfa.gov.sg/content/mfa/countries_and_region/northeast_asia/prc.printable.html?status=1.

including excessive consumption of resources, a widening gap between the rich and poor and serious environmental pollution due to the rapid economic development of previous years. The emphasis thus shifted to comprehensive, coordinated and sustainable development. A similar shift was also evident in Hu's concept of Harmonious Society endorsed by the Sixth Plenum of the 16th Communist Party of China Central Committee in 2006. A key tenet of this concept is a society where humans live in harmony with nature and the environment.

The Tianjin Eco-city is positioned as a "thriving city which is socially harmonious, environmentally-friendly and resource-efficient—a model for sustainable development". These are known as the "Three Harmonies" with people living in harmony with other people, i. e. social harmony; people living in harmony with economic activities, i. e. economic vibrancy; and people living in harmony with the environment, i. e. environmental sustainability.

The 30 km^2 Tianjin Eco-city is built on what is largely saltpan, barren land and polluted water-bodies, including a 2.6 km^2 large wastewater pond. ①A conscious decision was made not

① This pond, known as Jing Lake, has now been cleaned up and boast a vibrant marine life. See "Tianjin Eco-city a role model: Tharman", *Straits Times*, 26 June 2017.

to build on precious arable land already in short supply due to land degradation and the challenge of feeding more people who are increasingly migrating to urban areas in China. By building on non-arable land and in an area known for water shortage, the Tianjin Eco-city seeks to underscore the message that it is possible to overcome these geographical limitations with existing technology and capabilities.

Another message that the Tianjin Eco-city seeks to convey is that modern, urban, high-density living is an affordable proposition based on present day eco-friendly practices and features. The Key Performance Indicators of the Eco-city bears this out. For instance, all buildings in the Eco-city meet the Green Building Evaluation Standards, a hybrid evaluation standard that combines China's Green Star with Singapore's Green Mark Certification. The public green space are set to be at least 12 square metres per person, the current standard in China. Water from all taps should be potable, a Singapore standard. To ensure that the Eco-city is not just an enclave of the rich but is open to people from all walks of life, the goal of having at least 20% of residential units to be developed as affordable public housing was set.

One indication of the relevance of the Eco-city to China's

development priorities was China's State Council designation of the Eco-city as China's first National Green Development Demonstration Zone (NGDDZ) in March 2013 and, thereafter in October 2014, China further announced preferential policies in industrial development, revenue and tax, finance, resource and environment management, and social governance to support the Eco-city's development. ①This is recognition that the development of the Eco-city will continue to shed valuable lessons and experience for China in its urbanisation and industrialization drive. Another indication that Tianjin Eco-city is making a positive contribution is that officials from the Xiongan New Area, a new area designated by President Xi Jinping to showcase the vision of high-quality urbanization for Beijing, Tianjin and Hebei, have visited the Eco-city to explore possible lessons especially in the ecological development aspects for the development of Xiongan New Area. ②

Furthermore, in July 2018, Singapore's Minister for National Development and Second Minister for Finance Lawrence Wong

① "Zhongguo Xinjiapo Tianjin shengtaicheng jianshe guojia lushe fazhan shifanqu shishi fang'an", *National Development and Reform Council*, 22 October 2014.

② "Shang Daman: Zhongxin Tianjin shengtaicheng jiang jinru qifei jieduan guaidian", *Lianhe Zaobao*, 26 June 2017.

and Tianjin Binhai New Area Party Secretary Zhang Yuzhuo officially launched the city centre of the Tianjin Eco-city to mark the Eco-city's next phase of development. In this phase, the focus will be on completing projects like the transit hub (including a rail line station and bus interchange), gateway plaza (comprising office towers, hotels, residential buildings, and convention and exhibition facilities), a Sino-Singapore Friendship Garden (which will have a tropical greenhouse to showcase Singapore's "City in a Garden" concept and will display a collection of tropical gardens and plants) and a Sino-Singapore Friendship Library (which will be the largest library in the Eco-city). ①These projects when completed, will enhance the appeal of the Eco-city as a place to work, live and play in.

(c) Chongqing Connectivity Initiative (CCI)

While the SIP and Tianjin Eco-city are confined to a particular location and making that location as attractive as possible, the third G-to-G project goes well beyond a particular geographical location. While location is still important, what is

① "Development of the Sino-Singapore Tianjin Eco-city Moves to City Centre", *Singapore's Ministry of National Development*, 1 July 2018.

even more important is to link that particular location/node, i. e. Chongqing where the project is sited, with as many other locations/nodes as possible. The emphasis is thus on building connectivity and synergies rather than focusing on a particular site.

The idea for Singapore and China to collaborate on a third G-to-G was reportedly first raised by Vice Premier Zhang Gaoli when he came to Singapore in October 2013 to attend the 10th Joint Council for Bilateral Cooperation (JCBC), a high level body that oversees cooperation between the two countries. The two sides deliberated further on this project at the 11th and 12th JCBC in October 2014 and October 2015 respectively. The project, with a base in Chongqing, was announced during President Xi Jinping's state visit to Singapore in November 2015 which also marked the 25th anniversary of diplomatic relations.

To be sure, after the SIP and Tianjin Eco-city projects, the Singapore government had indicated that it would not readily embark on a third G-to-G project in China. In fact, Singapore's PM Lee Hsien Loong reportedly said in 2010 that "future bilateral business ventures in China should be driven by Singapore companies rather than the Singapore government, which will play more of a supporting role". ①An

① "S'pore to Let Firms Take Lead in China", *Straits Times*, 12 October 2010.

oft-cited reason, it seems, has been that as a small country, Singapore does not have enough resources to enter into several high level cooperation projects with China. Another less obvious but equally important reason is the huge political risks involved in such high profile projects. More specifically, by lending their names or reputation to these projects, the two governments have a primary and heavy responsibility to ensure that the projects succeed. A successful project will have a positive impact on bilateral relations. Conversely, if they are not successful, the projects will produce an unintended opposite effect which can become a liability in the bilateral relationship.

Hence, when news that Singapore and China was exploring a third G-to-G project was first made public sometime in 2014, the Singapore side emphasized that this was a request mooted by the Chinese side. It is reasonable to conclude that Vice Premier Zhang would not have made such a request without approval from President Xi Jinping. From the Singapore perspective, for the project to have a fair chance to succeed, it had to be in line with Beijing's development priorities and be fully supported by the local authorities. In an indication that these two criteria were met, it was announced during Xi's visit in November 2015 that the CCI was "the key priority demonstration project" between the two countries under China's BRI, Western Region Development and Yangtze River Economic Belt strategies. ①

Another indispensable criterion for CCI success is that the project had to be commercially viable, similar to the two previous G-to-G projects. However, unlike the SIP and Tianjin Eco-city which are located in Suzhou and Tianjin respectively, the emphasis of the CCI is less on its physical location (although its base is in Chongqing) and more on establishing "modern connectivity and modern services". In other words, the focus is on establishing connectivity (within and beyond Chongqing) and promoting collaboration in specific industries.

Under CCI, four priority areas of cooperation have been identified, i. e. financial services, aviation, transport and logistics, and ICT. These are areas where Singapore's strengths lie and where China is also keen to develop. When the two sides met for the second Joint Implementation Committee meeting in September 2016, they discussed a draft Chongqing Transport and Logistics Master Plan that articulated a vision to develop

---

① "Joint statement between the People's Republic of China and the Republic of Singapore on the establishment of an All-Round Cooperative Partnership Progressing with the Times", *Singapore's Ministry of Foreign Affairs*, 7 November 2015.

Chongqing into a multi-modal hub of Western China. The proposed master plan also included information connectivity which is a key enabler to improve logistics efficiency in both regional and global trade flows. In the financial sector, it was further announced that Singapore and Chinese financial institutions have signed more than US $6 billion (S $8.16 billion) worth of financial services deals since its launch in November 2015. ①In the aviation sector, Changi Airports International is working with Chongqing Airport Group to manage the non-aeronautical business of Chongqing Airport including retail, food and beverage, VIP complex, car park, duty free shops and advertising. ②Aviation connectivity between Singapore and Chongqing has also significantly increased from five flights to 14 flights per week. ③

To further promote CCI's connectivity, the CCI-Southern Transport Corridor (CCI-STC) was proposed and established under the CCI in 2017. The purpose of this corridor is to link

① "Singapore, China 'Very Happy' with Progress of Chongqing Connectivity Initiative: Chan Chun Sing", *Channel News Asia*, 1 September 2016.

② "Singapore & Chongqing Successfully Conclude First Joint Implementation Committee Meeting for Chongqing Connectivity Initiative", *Singapore's Ministry of Trade and Industry*, 8 January 2016.

③ "Minister (PMO) Chan Chun Sing's Oral Reply on the Chongqing Connectivity Initiative Project", *Singapore's Ministry of Trade and Industry*, 19 March 2018.

Chongqing to Qinzhou (in the Beibu Gulf of Guangxi province) in the south by rail and the reafter from Qinzhou to Singapore and beyond by sea, thereby enhancing multi-modal connectivity between Western China, Southeast Asia and the rest of the world (see picture overleaf). President Xi Jinping has reportedly referred to the CCI-STC as the international land and sea corridor that connects the overland Silk Road Economic Belt with the 21st Century Maritime Silk Road. ①

The more established route is for goods from Chongqing to travel west-ward along the Yangtze River all the way to Shanghai before they are exported to the rest of the world. Offering an alternative, the CCI-STC will reduce the amount of time needed to transport goods between Chongqing and Singapore to about a week, which is a third of today's usual route and will result in savings in logistic costs for businesses and companies. Since December 2017, three block train services have been commissioned between Chongqing and Guangxi per week. To further promote seamless rail-sea connectivity between Western China and Southeast Asia, Singapore's port operator Port of

① "Minister (PMO) Chan Chun Sing's Oral Reply on the Chongqing Connectivity Initiative Project", *Singapore's Ministry of Trade and Industry*, 19 March 2018.

Singapore Authority (PSA), home-grown shipping line Pacific International Lines (PIL) and IBM Singapore conducted a trial run of a block chain-based supply chain platform to track and trace cargo movement from Chongqing to Singapore via the CCI-STC from August 2017 to February 2018. Moving beyond the trial phase, the three partners are now looking to engage more participants from the different nodes of the distribution network that form the supply chain logistics eco-system. ①Going forward, businesses and companies can choose the type of multimodal transport that best suit them.

In any endeavor, there are bound to be challenges. One of the key challenges in building the CCI-STC is to break away from the traditional mind set of just promoting a particular location without due or much regard for other locations to one where joint promotion of different locations, and leveraging on the strengths and comparative advantages of these different locations, could be available and cost effective way of doing business. It is with this in mind that both Chongqing and Singapore have adopted an open and inclusive approach for other Chinese provinces to come on

① "PIL, PSA and IBM concluded a successful blockchain trial from Chongqing to Singapore via the Southern Transport Corridor", *Pacific International Lines News Release*, 23 February 2018.

board. So far, apart from Chongqing, Guangxi, Guizhou and Gansu have officially come on board.

In another positive development, at a joint meeting held in Chongqing in April 2018, Chongqing, Guangxi, Guizhou and Gansu invited six other provinces and autonomous regions, namely Inner Mongolia, Sichuan, Yunnan, Shaanxi, Qinghai and Xinjiang, to jointly issue a Chongqing Declaration（重庆倡议）. The declaration indicated the commitment of the 10 provinces and autonomous regions to support the development of the CCI-STC.①Certainly, the expression of official support by the 10 provinces and autonomous region is most welcomed and the next step is to translate this expression of political support into concrete actions on the ground in support of the CCI-STC.

The other challenge is to get more companies and businesses to work on the four identified priority areas as well as use the CCI-STC since the success of the CCI-STC goes beyond just official support. In fact, the best indicator of CCI-STC success is when more and more businesses and companies use this corridor which will in turn reduce overall cost for users. Before the CCI-STC,

① "Xibu shi shengqu tichu ‘Chongqing changyi’ gongjian Zhongxin hezuo nanxiang tongdao", *China's Ministry of Commerce*, 23 April 2018.

existing business and companies have already established their respective product supply chains and logistical networks. Hence, trying to convince more businesses and companies to try out the CCI-STC will require time and effort. They will only do so if it makes commercial sense.

A representative from a seafood company interested in the CCI-STC told the author that potential Chinese clients in Chongqing already have established product supply chains with their respective suppliers in China's coastal areas and that these suppliers also have the necessary warehouse facilities to handle a large volume of seafood cargo. At the moment, all that the Chinese clients need to do is to make a call on what type and volume of seafood they require and this will be delivered straight to him in no time. The Chinese clients do not need to worry about anything else, least of all the logistical arrangements involved in transporting the seafood. For the CCI-STC to rival this arrangement, it would have to offer businesses and companies seamless and cost-effective logistical service from source to delivery.

Another representative from a paper and pulp company in Southeast Asia remarked that there is huge demand for pulp from his Chinese clients. According to this representative, the pulp that he delivers to his clients in Chongqing still has to overcome some logistical bottlenecks which add to the overall transaction costs. If these logistical kinks can be sorted out, which would require close collaboration between the local authorities and businesses, then it will certainly help to make his business more viable. ①

Some Observations

Way before BRI, Singapore and China have already engaged in building connectivity with each other through practical and hands-on cooperation such as in the form of G-to-G projects. Singapore is among the handful of countries that has such G-to-G projects with China. Apart from the bilateral connectivity arising from collaboration on these projects, there is multilateral connectivity involved as well since these projects require the participation of other actors/players especially international and foreign companies and businesses for them to pass the test of success.

The first G-to-G project in the form of the SIP helped to connect China to international business and capital by offering a

① Interviews with respective company representatives in August 2018.

platform where foreign and local companies can enjoy the convenience of one-stop service. This connectivity was important because at that time China had few friends, was short of capital and needed a platform to attract foreign companies to create jobs for growth. Today, this connectivity remains important as the SIP strives to stay ahead of the competition through industrial upgrading and urbanisation. Taking references from external experience and best practices else where is a strong manifestation of connectivity at work. Singapore has also continued to share its software experience with China till this day. The second G-to-G project sought to offer green, smart yet affordable solutions to urban living in the form of the Tianjin Eco-city. It is meant as a reference point to address environmental pollution in China and offer a proposition that is in harmony with people, with economic activities and the environment. Like SIP, apart from sharing urban solutions practiced in Singapore and China, the two countries also welcome urban best practices and solutions from around the world.

The CCI is the third and most recent G-to-G project that is specifically identified as related to China's BRI. The connectivity in this project can be viewed from several aspects. There is connectivity in terms of bringing companies and businesses to collaborate with each other in the four areas of transport and logistics, financial services, aviation and ICT. There is also connectivity in linking Chongqing with other provinces in Western China and even westwards to other countries through the Silk Road Economic Belt. Furthermore, there is connectivity in linking Chongqing to other parts of Southeast Asia and beyond via the CCI-STC. In this sense, the STC part has a strategic element to it in that it links the overland Silk Road Economic Belt with the Maritime Silk Road. In terms of the modalities of connectivity, the emphasis is on multimodal freight connectivity whether it is land, air, sea or rail. There is also digital connectivity involved such as the use of block chain technology to facilitate the handling of freight that involves multimodal types of transport.

Without a doubt, building connectivity via the CCI-STC will require perseverance, time and effort. The participation of as many Chinese provinces and autonomous regions is important as the local authorities support is critical to facilitate cross-border transfer of goods and services, reduce non-tariff barriers and contribute in building a multimodal transport system. Equally important, if not more so, is the participation of businesses and companies not only in the four highlighted areas of cooperation but also in using the multimodal transport system. The best litmus test of the CCI-STC is when more and more businesses and companies endorse it by participating in it.

China – Southeast Asia Relations: Opportunities and Challenges

Deth Sok Udom *

China and the countries in Southeast Asia have shared a long history of social, economic, and political relations. Partly thanks to the economic connections between Sino-Southeast Asians and their mainland counterparts, but also because of China's rise as an economic powerhouse, China has become a major trading partner with ASEAN countries. With a trade volume of $514.82 billion in 2017, China has remained the largest trade partner of ASEAN for the ninth year in a row, which is 6.6 times the size of trade

* Deth Sok Udom is President of Zaman University, Cambodia.

volume in 2003, when the two sides established strategic partnership.[①] Apart from trade, increasing investments and infrastructure projects prior to or as part of the Belt and Road Initiatives have also increased dramatically between China and ASEAN countries. As Yoon Ah observed, during the past decade, "China has emerged as a key partner of Southeast Asia (SEA) across trade, investment, and infra-structure development".[②]

The recently escalating trade war between the United States and China, however, has added interesting dynamics to China – Southeast economic relations. Thanks to the rising tariffs on products manufactured in China, several companies (Chinese or otherwise) are considering moving their production to some ASEAN countries such as Thailand, Malaysia and Vietnam, which have the capability and supply chain logistics to absorb the re-routing of investments in manufacturing sector. While this may

① Tan Xinyu, "China remains ASEAN's largest trade partner for ninth year", *China Daily*. Accessed on 22 December 2018 at http://www.chinadaily.com.cn/a/201807/18/WS5b4eb49ea310796df4df72d8.html. Data from the ASEAN Secretariat, however, puts the figure of total trade at only $441.6 billion.

② Yoon Ah, "China's Economic Ties with Southeast Asia," *World Economy Brief*, Vol. 7, No. 8 (September 2017): p. 1. Accessed on 22 December 2018 at https://think-asia.org/bitstream/handle/11540/7468/WEB%2017-18.pdf?sequence=1.

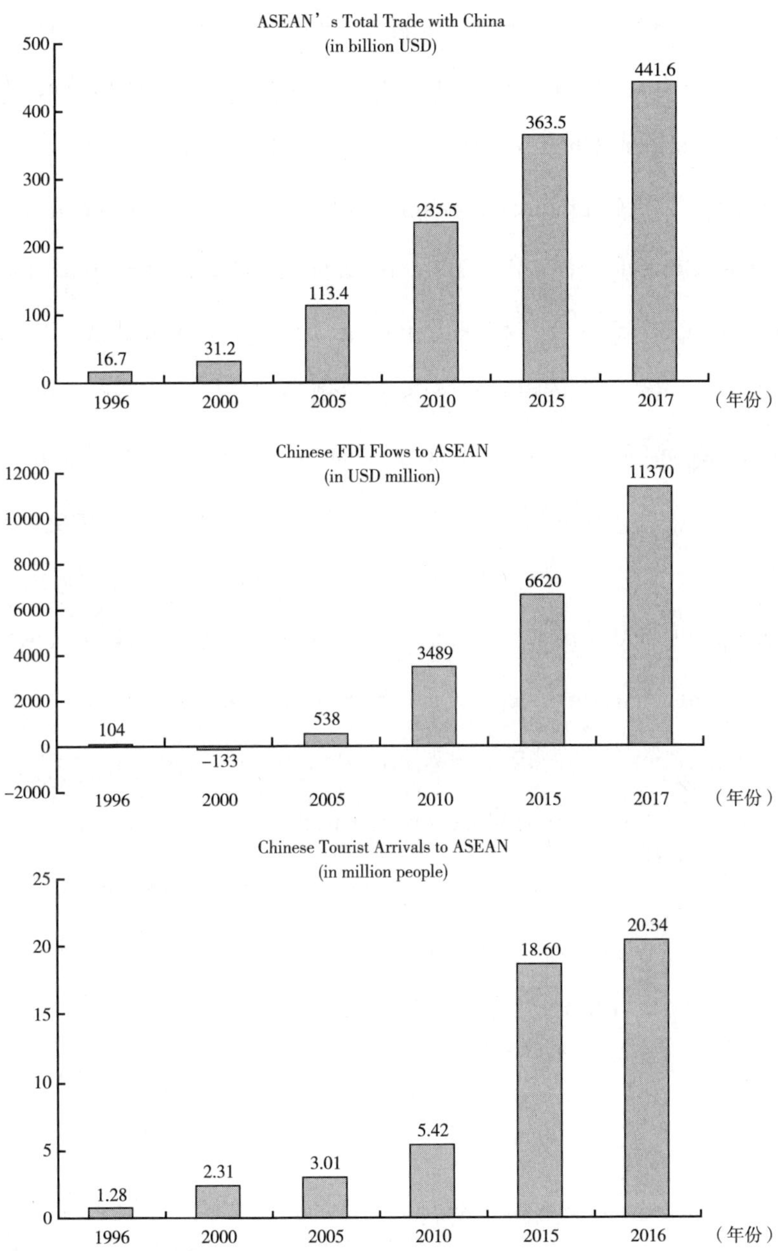

(Source: ASEAN Focus, Issue 6/2018, p. 13)

increase investments from China to Southeast Asia, it raises the questions for China's domestic reliance on manufacturing sector. The American Chamber of Commerce China and the American Chamber of Commerce Shanghai, for instance, estimated that "approximately one-third of more than 430 American companies in China have or are considering moving their production bases elsewhere to negate the effects of tariffs". ①But while certain countries in Southeast Asia could benefit from such relocation of factories, the overall prospect for global trade could be grim. As Gnanasagaran suggested, "In the long term, a prolonged trade war spells bad news as countries engage in retaliatory measures which then lead to a downward spiral of confrontation. After all, the net effect of a trade war is that global trade contracts will deal a blow to the primarily export-oriented economies of Southeast Asia". ② On a more optimistic note, Moeller posited that the long-term, indirect, effects of the trade war on Southeast Asia would be as follows:

① Angaindrankumar Gnanasagaran, "Southeast Asia: Victors of the trade war?" (4 October 2018), *The ASEAN Post.* Accessed on 23 December 2018, https://theaseanpost.com/article/southeast-asia-victors-trade-war.

② Ibid.

· Southeast Asian exports of intermediate goods to China will be hit, but the trade war may lead to U. S. demand for Southeast Asian goods replacing imports from China.

· The indirect, long-term positive effect will be a stronger and faster switch from global to a regional supply chains auguring a more self-sustaining Asian economy. ①

It remains to be seen how the trade war will continue to affect relations between China and Southeast Asia.

Apart from economic relations, however, political and social relations between China and Southeast Asians are somewhat more complicated. Different ASEAN countries with different histories of foreign affairs have different histories and dynamics when it comes to their dealings with China. Nonetheless, the different cases discussed in this paper offer similar points for consideration for China's decision makers in regards to how to achieve long-term and beneficial relationships with ASEAN countries. We shall briefly examine the cases of the Philippines, Malaysia, and

---

① Joergen Oerstroem Moeller, "U. S. -China Trade War: Opportunities & Risks for Southeast Asia," *ISEAS Perspectives*, No. 64 (October 2018), p. 1.

Cambodia, to discuss the complexities and factors that needed to be taken into consideration when viewing China and Southeast Asia through non-economic lenses.

The Philippines and China have held centuries-long economic relations in their histories. Yet, the Philippines' traditional alliance with the United States since the outset of the Cold War, as well as the dispute over the Spratly islands in the South China Sea meant that relations in the modern time have not been always amicable. Relations between the two countries reached a low point when the Philippines under former President Aquino Jr. began processing a case at the arbitration tribunal against Chinese claims in the South China Sea in 2013. The election of Duterte, however, reversed the course of the two countries' ties, as the new Philippines president downplayed the tribunal's ruling in favor of the Philippines and sought closer economic ties with China. The past two years have witnessed warmer relations, and increasing number of trade deals between both countries, with total trade volume now exceeding USD 50 billion. In the latest state visit by President Xi Jinping to the Philippines in November 2018, 29 MOUs of cooperation were signed. Despite the warming of government-to-government relations, challenges remain. As Liang Fook pointed out, Duterte has to grapple not only with a domestic backlash which was already apparent during Xi's visit to the Philippines, but also how to maintain a good balance as a country coordinator of China - ASEAN relations for the next three years. ①Fook further suggested that:

> It is as much in the Philippines' interest to adopt a more neutral foreign policy orientation vis-à-vis China as it is for China to pursue a relationship with the Philippines that is not solely dependent on China dolling out benefits. A situation where each other's independence and sovereignty is seen as being respected and safeguarded especially from the domestic angle would make for a more lasting and stable relationship. ②

The recommendation should be given serious thought, especially in the lights of apparent recent slowdown in Malaysia - China relations under Prime Minister Mahathir following his electoral victory in May 2018. As of August 2018, for instance,

---

① Lye Liang Fook, "China - Philippine Relations and Xi Jinping's State Visit: Context, Significance and Challenges", *ISEAS Perspective* No. 81 (December 2018): p. 6.

② Ibid., p. 7.

PM Mahathir has already canceled the Chinese-funded East Coast Rail Link, which his predecessor Najib Razak had claimed would bring prosperity to eastern Malaysia. Bloomberg Opinion columnist Andy Mukherjee rightly observed that, Mahathir's cancellations or freezing of various Chinese projects show that "sovereignty-and Malaysia's racial politics-are Mahathir's real concerns". ①

Cambodia presents another interesting case of China-Southeast Asia relations. Cambodia under Prince Sihanouk was among the first in the region to recognize the People's Republic of China in 1958. Relations fluctuated during the ensuing decades as Cambodia went through frequent regime changes thanks to both domestic politics and the Cold War impacts on the Indochina region. Starting from 1997, and especially during the last decade, Cambodia's relations with China have strengthened both economically and politically. ②With a trade volume worth over

---

① Andy Mukherjee, "No Chinese Belt, Road or Bedrooms for Mahathir's Malaysia", Bloomberg Opinion (28 August 2018). Accessed on 23 December 2018 at https://www.washingtonpost.com/business/no-chinese-belt-roador-bedroomsfor-mahathirs-malaysia/2018/08/28/57c6c7ea-ab2b-11e8-9a7d-cd30504ff902_story.html? utm_term=.f6ecc596ec09.

② For a comprehensive discussion on Cambodia-China relations, see Cheunboran Chanborey, "Cambodia-China Relations: What Do Cambodia's Past Strategic Directions Tell Us?", in Deth Sok Udom, Sun Suon & Serkan Bulut (eds.), *Cambodia's Foreign Relations in Regional Global Contexts* (Phnom Penh: KAS Cambodia, 2017).

USD 5 billion, China is Cambodia's top trading partner. China is also the top source of foreign direct investments and tourists in Cambodia, as well as a major donor for the country. In marking the 60th anniversary of relationship between the two countries, Cambodia's Ministry of Foreign Affairs and International Cooperation released three letters from King Norodom Sihamoni, Prime Minister Hun Sen and Foreign Affairs minister Prak Sokhonn. The King, for his part, noted "with great satisfaction the growing political trust and official exchanges at all levels between our two countries, and highly appreciate the cordial hospitality accorded to me and our Queen Mother every time we visit China", while Prime Minister Hun Sen's letter praised China for being a major donor to Cambodia and the biggest source of foreign direct investment. ① Foreign Minister Prak Sokhonn, likewise, praised the Belt and Road Initiative in Cambodia, which include the Phnom Penh-Sihanoukville express way and planned new airports in Siem Reap province and Phnom Penh, among others. ②But despite the close ties between governments, the same

① Niem Chheng, "King, PM, minister celebrate China ties", *Phnom Penh Post* (20 July 2018). Accessed on 23 December 2018 at https://www.phnompenhpost.com/national/king-pm-minister-celebrate-china-ties.

② Ibid.

cannot be said for people-to-people relations. Recently, resentment among Cambodians against the influx of Chinese presence is apparent. The occasional news of fatal traffic accidents caused by Chinese drivers and street fights with involvement of Chinese gangsters put Chinese presence in Cambodia in a bad light. Likewise, the case of Sihanoukville, a once-sleepy coastal town in the southwest of Cambodia which has been radically transformed by the sudden influx of Chinese casinos and constructions (dubbed the "New Macau" by some), demonstrates how local resentment can arise as a result of the social vice, infrastructure problems, and changing dynamics of the town. Sihanoukville has also garnered international media attention as a "bad example" of Chinese investments. ①

Apart from country-specific issues, China in general suffers from a soft power deficit, and its rise has created nervousness to varying degrees among its neighbors. As Steven Wong pointed out, "Closer to home, its island-building and militarisation of the South China Sea, which it perceives as essential for security, has

① See, for example, " 'No Cambodia left': how Chinese money is changing Sihanoukville", *The Guardian* (31 July 2018). Accessed on 23 December 2018 at https://www.theguardian.com/cities/2018/jul/31/no-cambodia-left-chinese-money-changing-sihanoukville.

built it little trust and won it few friends from within and outside the region". ①Increasing trade deficit has also caused some ASEAN member states' concerns over the loss of competitiveness, over-dependence, and debt to China. ②

Conclusion

Relations between China and Southeast Asia are on the rise, especially in economic and political aspects. But such increases also create social problems, and in some cases, perception by many Southeast Asians toward China's as having "over-presence" and seeking "hegemonic ambitions" in the region. The example from the Philippines, Malaysia and Cambodia suggest that it is imperative that China's engagements with Southeast Asia are done in such a way that local populations do not become victims of China's economic presence, lest these become recipes for anti-Chinese sentiments and spiral into political effects that may be difficult to manage regardless of how close governments'

① Steven Wong, "ASEAN Braces For a Risen China", *ASEAN Focus* (Issue 6/2018), p. 2. Accessed on 23 December 2018 at https://www.iseas.edu.sg/images/pdf/ASEANFocus_December2018_Final.pdf.

② Ibid., p. 3.

relationships are on the elite-level. After all, China and ASEAN need each other to grow in the long run. As advised by Steven Wong: "China does need to calibrate its relationship better, building more trust and giving more benefit to the region, but this can only happen in the context of an established and growing relationship. Whatever tests and challenges the ASEAN-China relationship face, little is to be practically gained from a distancing from each other, much less as bandwagoning rivals."①

① Steven Wong, "ASEAN Braces For a Risen China", *ASEAN Focus* (Issue 6/2018), p. 2. Accessed on 23 December 2018 at https://www.iseas.edu.sg/images/pdf/ASEANFocus_December2018_Final.pdf.

东盟多边外交战略的演变、特点及挑战[*]

毕世鸿[**]

摘　要： 冷战后，东盟实施多边外交战略，采取多头下注和风险对冲等策略，在大国间开展大国平衡外交。为提升多边外交战略的有效性以维持东盟的中心性和整体性，东盟在加强自身能力建设的同时，通过主导众多多边合作机制，增强与大国、地区组织和国际组织的双/多边合作关系，加快实施海洋安全等各功能领域的行动计划，扩大和其他地区组织、机制之间的合作，提升了其在亚太地区和全球性问题上的影响力，从而将以

* 本文是以下基金项目的阶段性成果：2017 年度教育部哲学社会科学研究重大课题攻关项目“‘一带一路’背景下中国特色周边外交理论与实践创新研究”（17JZD035）、2016 年度国家社科基金特别委托项目（16@ZH009）、云南大学 2018 年度边疆治理与地缘政治学科（群）特区高端科研成果培育项目（Z2018－04）、“云南大学一流大学建设周边外交研究理论创新高地项目”、“国家级高端智库与教育部新型智库培育建设（周边外交研究中心）”项目。

** 毕世鸿，云南大学周边外交研究中心、国际关系研究院、“一带一路”研究院教授，博士生导师。

东盟为中心的点线结构构建成立体多维结构。但东盟在大国间的摇摆、内部协调不一致等问题也会影响东盟多边外交战略的实施。在亚太地区大国均无力建立地区霸权的格局下，东盟虽无力解决大国间的纷争，却能在一定程度上防止大国间紧张关系的升级，对过渡期的亚太地区国际关系起到稳定阀的作用。

关键词： 东盟　多边外交战略　中心性　大国平衡

当前，在全球化进程不断推进的国际社会中，构建排他性地区组织或合作机制已不合时宜。各地区组织在不断加强域内合作的同时，也在探索如何加强与大国的合作。无论是从促进经济和社会发展的视角，还是实现地区和平与安全的视角，东盟在建设政治安全、经济和社会文化三大共同体的过程中，深化域内合作和加强与大国的合作同等重要。但大国间的权力转移及随之而来的大国竞争，正深刻地影响着亚太地区国际关系。作为中小国家集团，东盟正在艰难探索，试图建立更加符合自身利益的亚太地区新秩序。通过设立东盟地区论坛（ARF）、“10＋1”、“10＋3”、东亚峰会（EAS）、东盟防长扩大会议（“ADMM＋”）等多边合作机制，东盟不断加强与中美日印澳等大国在各功能领域的合作，建立起了以其为中心的复杂的地区合作机制网络，并在上述机制中发挥了主导作用。

值得注意的是，东盟不断加强与大国的合作在客观上也造成大国在亚太国际政治空间中的比重不断提高。当大国竞争加剧时，东盟如何应对？新加坡的前高级外交官曾围绕这个问题爆发了激烈的争论。[①] 马凯硕认为小国应坚持小国的立场，应谨慎对待涉及大国利益的重要问题。[②] 比拉哈里·考西坎和王景荣等则认为，即便是小国，对于与本国利益密切相关的问题也要发出声音。正因为如此，新加坡才能受到国际社会的尊敬。在大国竞争中保持沉默并不明智，反而是危险的。[③] 尚穆根也主张："我们应该明确国家的核心利益，并通过巧妙方式实现，但绝不是卑躬屈膝的方式"。[④] 之所以引发此类争论，源于卡塔尔被中东周边大国孤立。中美日印澳等大国竞争加剧，使新加坡感受到了巨大压力。[⑤] 当前，围绕亚太地区安

① Engseng Ho, "Small states on the superpower seesaw," *The Strait Times*, July 6, 2017.

② Kishore Mahbubani, "Qatar: Big lessons from a small country," *The Strait Times*, July 2, 2017.

③ BilahariKausikan, "Singapore cannot be cowed by size," *The Strait Times*, July 3, 2017.

④ 包雪琳：《"小国大外交"卡塔尔断交风波触动新加坡》，新华网，2017年7月9日，http://news.xinhuanet.com/world/2017-07/09/c_129650483.htm。

⑤ Mushahid Ali, "China's Hegemonic Trajectory: Intimidating ASEAN?", *RSIS Commentary*, No. 245, October 4, 2016.

全、经济合作、南海争端、国际规则、基础设施建设等诸多问题，东南亚更成为大国博弈和竞争的重要舞台。

迄今，学界针对东盟的对外关系开展了诸多研究。一些学者把东盟国家的外交战略逻辑与地位放在冷战后秩序变迁与成员国“弱者”身份的前提下进行探讨。① 但在研究亚太地区国际关系时，还有一个不可忽视的因素即中小国家与大国的关系。菊池努指出东盟虽然实力较弱，但对大国关系和亚太地区国际关系的发展方向也会产生影响。肖欢容、张锡镇指出东盟开展平衡外交战略，是利用各大国的优势以实现大国在东南亚的势力均衡，维护地区安全与稳定。安东尼认为东盟构建了一系列以己为核心的区域机制框架，在议程倡议与理念引导方面发挥引领作用。李鼎鑫等指出东盟以离岸“平衡手”的身份开展大国外交，最大限度地提升自身的博弈地位和战略利益。王玉主认为东盟通过对时局的充分把握，发挥自身作为区域组织的优势和能动性，谋求更有利的国际地位。魏玲、喻常森指出东盟的大国外交是平衡和网络构建，即本土规范扩散、国际规范本土化和大国社会化。李红等认为在“东盟－东亚－亚太”的多层次地缘政治空间中，处于弱势的东盟通过提升网络中介作用开展大国外交。韦红强调以东盟为中心、域外大国

① David Martin Jones & Michael L. R. Smith, “Making Process, Not Progress: ASEAN and the Evolving East Asian Regional Order,” *International Security*, Vol. 32, No. 1, 2007.

为借力的多层次的安全合作机制被东盟赋予了重要的安全意义。山影进认为东盟外交战略有不让大国参与和让各大国参与并相互牵制的两种考量，这两种线路并行不悖并延续至今。①上述成果为本研究提供了有益参考。

对于东盟而言，如何应对大国间权力转移是其外交政策的重要课题，这将在一定程度上左右未来亚太地区国际关系的走向。东盟出台的文件多次强调要保持其“中心性”，以保持自身的独立自主和整体性，这反映了东盟以多边主义为理念的多边外交战略的诉求。基于这一考量，东盟的多边外交战略采取多头下注策略和风险对冲等策略，不断推出新的多边合作机制，在大国间开展大国平衡外交。本文在论述东盟为维持其中心性和整体性而实施的多边外交

① 菊池努:「米中関係を超えて一大国間の権力政治と東南アジア」、『国際問題』、2017 年 10 月号、第 1 頁。张锡镇:《东盟实施大国平衡战略的新进展》,《东南亚研究》, 2008 年第 3 期。肖欢容、刘欣宜:《冷战后东盟的大国平衡战略》,《东南亚纵横》2009 年第 2 期。Mely Cabllere Anthony, “Understanding ASEAN Bases and Protects in Evolving Regional Architecture”, *The Pacific Review*, Vol. 27, No. 4, 2014. 李鼎鑫、黄蕙:《试论东盟平衡外交战略的四个维度》,《学习与探索》2014 年第 8 期。王玉主:《小国集团的能动性——东盟区域合作战略研究》,《当代亚太》2013 年第 3 期。魏玲:《关系平衡、东盟中心与地区秩序演进》,《世界经济与政治》2017 年第 7 期。喻常森:《智者不惑，强者必趋——简评〈国际政治中“弱者”逻辑——东盟与亚太地区大国关系〉》,《南洋问题研究》2011 年第 3 期。李红、覃巧玲:《基于网络视角的东盟地缘中心性战略环境分析》,《世界经济与政治论坛》, 2016 年第 2 期。韦红:《东盟海上安全合作机制: 路径、特征及困境分析》, 《战略决策研究》2017 年第 5 期。山影進:「クオヴァディス— ASEANへの問いかけ」、『国際問題』、2015 年 11 月号、第 2 頁。

战略演变历程的基础上，针对当前亚太地区形势，研究东盟实践多边外交战略的主要机制，论述其多边外交战略的指向、实践成效及特点，分析其面临的挑战。最后，阐明东盟的多边外交战略对于亚太地区今后国际关系走向所具有的重要意义。

一　东盟多边外交战略的演变

自独立以来，东盟国家在大国竞争乃至对立的严峻环境中建设国家，大国关系发生任何变化，都有可能使其再次被卷入大国竞争的漩涡之中。1967 年成立的东盟既是为了应对外部威胁，同时也是为了维持成员国的团结。[①] 而维系东盟国家的纽带，除了反帝国主义和反殖民主义以外，还有针对美国等大国垄断地区事务的焦虑以及保持独立自主性的诉求。其后，东盟国家借助东盟与大国开展对话，先后和日本、美国、加拿大、澳大利亚等国建立对话伙伴国机制。其目的在于，东盟国家不仅能够单独和大国开展双边外交，也能通过加强东盟组织的整体性来提升自身的谈判能力，同时避免某个大国对其施加影响力，继而形成大国之间的相互牵制。但在当时，东盟并不

① 曹云华主编《东南亚国家联盟——结构、运作与对外关系》，中国经济出版社，2011，第 7 页。

赞成加入多边合作机制。在20世纪70年代东盟倡导的东盟“和平、自由和中立区”构想中，曾明确反对大国介入东南亚国际关系。东盟甚至认为通过将大国排挤出东南亚，能够实现本地区的和平与稳定。东盟反对由日本提出的环太平洋经济圈构想以及美日澳提出的建设太平洋贸易发展组织，担心自身影响力由此降低，继而损害东盟的整体性并成为美日等大国控制东南亚事务的工具。①

冷战后，亚太地区政治安全环境发生沧海桑田的变化，东盟认识到让大国参与本地区合作进程是有利的，遂在保留独立自主性的同时，转而积极构建多边合作机制，甚至有意借助大国参与来构建自己所主导的新地区秩序。东盟国家虽然国情各异，也针对大国采取了加强双边关系的多头下注策略，从而与东盟采取的多边外交战略形成里外配合、互为表里的关系。据此，东盟利用对话伙伴国等机制，以“10+1”为主要抓手，大力拓展和加强与大国的关系。1994年，东盟创办ARF，该论坛是亚太地区首个针对政治安全对话的多边机制，也是东盟多边外交战略的首次实践。② 亚洲金融危机后，东盟发起成立了“10+3”机制，以推动东亚地区合作。

① 大庭三枝：『アジア太平洋地域形成への道程—境界国家日豪のアイデンティティ模索と地域主義—』京都：ミネルヴァ書房、2004、第280～283頁。

② Evan Berman & M. Shamsul Haque eds., *Asian Leadership in Policy and Governance*, Bingley: Emerald Insight Publisher, 2015, pp. 45–68.

EAS 自 2005 年启动，并逐渐发展成为以东盟为中心的多边合作机制。自 2010 年启动的“ADMM +”也是以 2006 年召开的东盟防长会议（ADMM）为基础，东盟邀请中国、美国、俄罗斯、日本、韩国、澳大利亚、新西兰和印度等国参加，亦成为其中心（见图 1）。上述合作机制的出台，体现了东盟通过实施多边外交战略不断升级与各大国双/多边关系的特点。

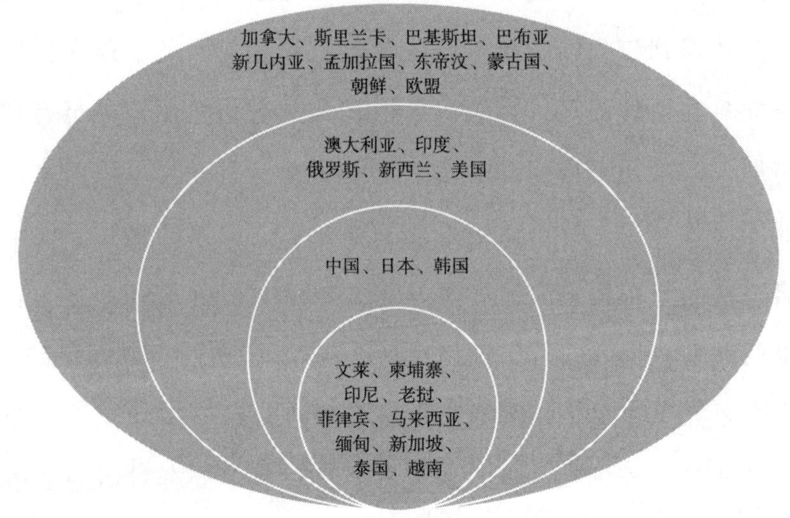

图 1　以东盟为中心的多边合作机制

此外，东盟与大国相继签署《东南亚友好合作条约》，促使大国接受东盟规范。自 2003 年以来，中国、印度、日本、澳大利亚、新西兰和美国等国相继签约。在经济领域，东盟最早与中国进行自贸区谈判。其后，东盟相继与日本、韩国、澳大利亚、新西兰和印度进行自贸区谈判，形成了以东盟为中心的自贸区网络。近年来，为了将上述“10+1”自贸区建成更为强大的多边自贸区，东盟与上述六国正式就缔结《区域全面经济伙伴关系》（RCEP）展开谈判，以东盟为中心的点线结构将由此演变为立体多维结构。①

随着以东盟为中心的多边合作机制网络的构建以及东盟和大国双/多边关系的不断增强，形成了大国间相互牵制的态势，东盟逐渐发展成为能够左右地区秩序的重要一极，继而实现把大国融入其所希望的地区秩序中这一目标。东盟之所以对大国采取上述策略，在于其独特的“大国平衡”论调及其外交理念。学界通常把“平衡”作为增强本国军事力量和加强与他国军事合作，继而对抗新兴势力的行动。但对于东盟国家而言，“大国平衡”的含义有所不同。② 一是大国已经深度介入东南亚国际关系体系之中。二是在追求本国和平与繁荣时，必须考虑大国的存在。三是在大国关系不透明的情况下，东盟国家应确保应对各种局面的灵活性。四是最能增强东盟国家对外谈判筹码的方式，在于避免卷入大国竞争，与所有大国维持友好关系并形成大国间的多边均衡状态。2013 年，时任印尼外

① 山影進：「ASEAN 外交半世紀にみる加盟国にとっての効用」、『国際問題』、2017 年 10 月号、第 4 頁。

② BilahariKausikan, “Standing up to and getting along with China,” *Today Online*, May 18, 2016, http://www.todayonline.com/chinaindia/standing-and-getting-along-china.

长马尔迪提出“富有魅力的平衡”战略，这印证了东盟国家为实现上述目的所采取的策略。[①]

对此，各大国不同程度地给予了尊重。美国奥巴马政府出台“亚太再平衡”战略的目的之一，就是加强对以东盟为中心的区域合作进程的介入力度。自特朗普执政以来，其在外交政策的发言中提及东盟的频率日益增多，不断邀请东盟国家领导人访美，或参加东盟系列峰会等。[②] 中国采取积极稳健的周边外交政策，通过建立战略合作伙伴关系、建设自由贸易区、共建“一带一路”、成立亚洲基础设施投资银行等方式不断加强与东盟国家的关系。日本历来重视发展与东盟及东盟国家的双多边关系，也在东盟发挥着独特的影响力。印度强调东盟在其“东进行动”战略中处于核心位置。在大国间没有形成零和博弈的情况下，东盟成为联系大国的纽带，并发挥了增信释疑的重要作用。

在东盟逐步占据亚太多边合作机制中心地位的过程中，东盟国家对构建东盟共同体的讨论也日益活跃。1976 年，东盟发表了宣布构建东盟共同体的《东盟协调一致宣言》。2003 年，东盟发表《东盟第二协调一致宣言》，规定东盟共

① Marty M. Natalegawa, “An Indonesian perspective on the Indo - Pacific,” Keynote address, CSIS, Washington D. C., May 16, 2013.

② Malcolm Cook, “Why now? Trump's Sudden Interest in Southeast Asia,” *The Interpreter*, May 3, 2017, https: //www. lowyinstitute. org/the - interpreter/why - now - trump - s - sudden - interest - southeast - asia.

同体由安全、经济和社会文化三大共同体组成。其后，东盟安全共同体改称东盟政治－安全共同体。在2009年出台的《东盟政治—安全共同体蓝图》（2015年蓝图）中，东盟强调在大国关系网中维持其“中心性”、构建以“10＋1”和东盟为中心的多边合作机制的重要性。[①] 这与2008年通过的《东盟宪章》所规定的外交战略一致。在2015年蓝图中，东盟确立了东盟政治－安全共同体的三大支柱，即一是建设拥有共同价值和规范且以制度为基础的共同体；二是建立在地区综合安全上承担共同责任，具有凝聚力、和平、稳定且具活力的地区；三是在一体化和相互依存的世界中保持活力和外向型的地区。[②] 上述三大支柱明确体现了东盟在政治安全领域实施多边外交战略的路径。

二 东盟多边外交战略的指向

在实施多边外交战略的过程中，东盟需要维持其“中心性”，即在“亚太地区多边合作框架中发挥中心作用”。关于这一考量，在2007年1月的东盟峰会发表的主席声明强调，

① ASEAN, *ASEAN Political－Security Community Blueprint*, Jakarta: ASEAN Secretariat, 2009.

② 《东盟政治—安全共同体蓝图（译文）》，王勤主编《东南亚地区发展报告（2014～2015）》，社会科学文献出版社，2015，第279页。

“对于本地区、国家和人民所面临的挑战和机遇，我们决心不断提升我们的立场，以维持东盟的中心性，并成为地区性引领力量和卓有成效的能够集体应对的推动力量”。[①] 在同年 11 月签署的《东盟宪章》第一条第十五款亦规定：“保持东盟中心性和积极的形象，体现其在与域外伙伴的合作关系中具备首屈一指的推动力，并在地区体系结构中展现其开放性、透明性以及包容性”。[②] 在 2010 年 3 月的东盟峰会主席声明中，对于如何维持东盟的“中心性”，亦有以下内容：“在正在形成的新的体系结构中，我们强调维持东盟中心作用的重要性及其决心。我们同意在两方面开展工作，即在重点加快东盟一体化和建设共同体的同时，加强东盟的对外关系，使其作为地区合作机制的推动力发挥应有的作用。我们强调必须与重要合作伙伴共同促进东盟的发展，对于重要的地区性问题和全球性问题形成东盟共通的立场和应对方法。我们同意，任何新的地区合作机制或议程原则上均是对现有多边机制和东盟中心性的有效补

① ASEAN, “Chairperson's Statement of the 12th ASEAN Summit ‘One Caring and Sharing Community,’” Cebu, Philippines, January 13, 2007, http://www.asean.org/news/item/chairperson-s-statement-of-the-12th-asean-summit-he-the-president-gloriamacapagal-arroyo-one-caring-and-sharing-community.

② ASEAN, “Charter of the Association of Southeast Asian Nations,” Singapore, November 20, 2007, http://www.asean.org/archive/publications/ASEAN-Charter.pdf.

充，并且是在其基础上发展而来的”。[①] 据此可知，“中心性”即东盟在 ARF、“10 + 3”、EAS、“ADMM + ”等多边合作机制中发挥中心作用和推动作用。此处的“中心作用”意味着东盟在多边合作机制的各级别会议、联合演习等活动中发挥引领作用。而“推动作用”则是指以东盟为主导，根据东盟制定的行动规范来逐步发展和扩大多边合作机制。

2015 年 11 月，东盟领导人会议宣布在同年底成立东盟三大共同体，并通过了愿景文件《东盟 2025：携手前行》（2025 年蓝图），东盟多边外交战略得到了全面更新，与 2015 年蓝图相比，堪称 2.0 升级版（见表 1）。

表 1　东盟 2015 年蓝图和 2025 年蓝图外交目标的比较

	2015 年蓝图	2025 年蓝图
东盟政治 - 安全共同体	目标：与世界紧密联系的富有魅力的开放性地区	目标：在富有魅力、开放性地区中保持东盟的中心性
	主要合作项目： 1. 维持东盟的中心性 2. 加强与区域外国家的关系 3. 加强在共同关心领域的合作	主要合作项目： 1. 增强东盟整体性和中心性 2. 加强与域外国家的关系

① ASEAN, “Chairman’s Statement of the 16th ASEAN Summit ‘Towards the ASEAN Community: from Vision to Action,’” Ha Noi, April 9, 2010, ttp: //www. asean. org/news/item/chairman - s - statement - of - the - 16th - asean - summit - towards - the - aseancommunity - from - vision - to - action.

续表

	2015 年蓝图	2025 年蓝图
东盟经济共同体	目标:融入全球经济一体化进程	目标:实现全球化的东盟
	主要合作项目: 1. 谋求发展对外经济关系 2. 加入全球产业链网络	主要合作项目: 1. 在对外经济关系上采取共同立场 2. 改进东盟自贸协定和投资促进计划 3. 加强与非自贸协定伙伴的经济合作 4. 与新兴经济体和地区组织建立伙伴关系 5. 支持多边贸易体系

资料来源：ASEAN, *ASEAN Political - Security Community Blueprint*, Jakarta: ASEAN Secretariat, 2009. ASEAN, *ASEAN* 2025: *Forging Ahead Together*, Jakarta: ASEAN Secretariat, 2015。

首先，2025 年蓝图明确了东盟政治 - 安全共同体的四个支柱，这比 2015 年蓝图增加了一个。这四个支柱，第一是建设基于原则、以人为中心的共同体；第二是在和平、安全、稳定的地区中建设具有活力的共同体；第三是开放性共同体；第四是加强制度引导，成为在地区和国际等层面不断增大影响力的共同体。其第一个支柱和 2015 年蓝图的第一个支柱“拥有共同价值和规范且以制度为基础的共同体”相比，根据东盟域内合作进展的成效制订了更为详细的行动计划，涵盖了人权、民主、自由、法制等领域。其他三个支柱则体现了东盟多边外交战略的目标指向。第三个支柱的“开放性共同体”更体现了东盟多边外交战略的具体路径，包括加强和大国的合作，在不断发展的地区合作框架中加强东盟的中心性，并为此制订了详细的行动计划。①

其次，2025 年蓝图强调在多边合作中加强东盟能力建设以及维持其中心性的必要性。在第三个支柱“开放性共同体”中，明确提出要加强东盟整体性及其中心性。在第二个支柱“在和平、安全、稳定的地区中建设具有活力的共同体”中，也一再强调东盟的中心性。在该支柱中，作为加强东盟能力建设的一环，加强 ARF 主席国作用的内容亦被提及。作为东盟主导的地区合作机制之一，ARF 原则上由东盟国家轮流担任主席国，以达到由东盟主导论坛议程的目的。同样，在“ADMM +”中，也有加强东盟中心性的项目。之所以出现以东盟为中心的诸多多边合作机制，也是由于各大国参与亚太地区国际政治机制化。据此，东盟国家进一步认识到增强自身发言权和影响力的重要性。

最后，2025 年蓝图宣布不仅在东盟一体化进程和亚太地区内增强东盟的作用，在针对各种全球性问题上也要提升东盟的影响力。对此，第三个支柱和第四个支柱均有提及。在第三个支柱中，为了能够在解决全球性问题上做出贡献，有必要加强东盟的能力建设。具体包括以下行动计划，一是为

① ASEAN, *ASEAN 2025: Forging Ahead Together*, Jakarta: ASEAN Secretariat, 2015.

了针对全球化进程中的重要问题提出解决的路径或施加影响，需要坚持东盟共同的立场。二是在东盟联合声明中针对重要问题提出统一见解。三是促进东盟和其他多边机制之间的协调。四是加强东盟国家间的调整，在可能的情况下，以东盟的名义推举候选人在多边合作机制中担任重要职位。第四个支柱要在东盟国家层面、地区层面和国际层面，进一步增强东盟的发言权。

三　东盟多边外交战略的具体实践及其成效

就东盟多边外交战略的整体而言，在以东盟为中心的各种合作机制中，东盟不仅要维持其中心性，还要推动制定东盟国家共同遵守的原则和规范，在和大国加强合作的同时不断扩大自身利益。换言之，该战略是对东盟迄今所采取的具体举措的一种事后承认。

在 2015 年蓝图中，上述第三个支柱“在全球化和相互依赖的世界中成为主动且外向型的地区”，从正面反映了东盟的中心性。为了夯实该支柱，东盟推出了“加强东盟中心性”的项目，并制订了具体的行动计划，即与对话伙伴国和其他大国利用“10＋1”、“10＋3”、EAS、ARF 等多边合作机制开展合作，举办各级别会议，担任会议的主席国、议长或共同议长。[①] 作为加强东盟中心性的一环，该文件还强调东盟国家要在对大国关系、地区和多边关系网络中进一步加强协调。而在制定2015年蓝图前，东盟就设立并举办了诸多高级别会议，诸如ARF、“10+1”和“10+3”领导人会议、EAS等均以东盟为中心。通过定期举办部长级会议和领导人会议，并由东盟和东盟国家作为议长或主席国主导会议议程，这在一定程度上维持了东盟的中心性。

其中，上述多边合作机制中，ARF和EAS较为典型地体现了东盟的“中心性”。目前，参与ARF这一多边合作机制的成员已经达到27个，其功能不仅局限于东盟成员国内部的对话、交流与协商，而且在于扩展与外部的安全合作与对话。ARF正使合作的水平不断提高，变成以行动为导向的论坛，其活动正迈向多样化，从学术会议到一般工作营、从沙盘推演到实地演习等，其合作领域和合作程度也正逐渐扩大并日益深化。[②] 自进入21世纪以来，中国、日本和韩国先后提出要与东盟共建关系紧密的东亚共同体等倡议，东盟对此欣然同意。但在正式举办EAS时，除了中、日、韩三国，东盟还邀请了澳大利亚、新西兰和印度加入，并将EAS变成各国领导人参

① ASEAN, *ASEAN Political - Security Community Blueprint*, Jakarta: ASEAN Secretariat, 2009.

② 赵海立：《东盟政治—安全共同体建设：成就与问题》，王勤主编《东南亚地区发展报告（2014～2015）》，社会科学文献出版社，2015，第34页。

与的外交论坛。东盟不仅借此维护了东盟协商一致的规范，坚持 EAS 的论坛性，也控制着 EAS 成员资格的门槛。通过对多边合作机制的引导，东盟在一定程度上有效化解了大国竞争，继而维护了东盟的中心性。①

自出台 2015 年蓝图后，东盟先后主办“ADMM +”和有关海洋安全的东盟海事论坛扩大会议（EAMF）等重要合作机制，进一步巩固了以东盟为中心的多边机制网络。“ADMM +”是在 2006 年召开的东盟防长会议基础上，邀请中国、日本、韩国、澳大利亚、新西兰、印度、美国和俄罗斯等 8 个对话伙伴国参加的多边合作机制。“ADMM +”首次会议于 2010 年 10 月举行，后于 2015 年 11 月和 2017 年 10 月先后举办了第 3 次和第 4 次会议。② “ADMM +”以非传统安全问题为中心，不断推进各功能领域的合作。具体而言，在人道主义援助和灾害救援、海洋安全、反恐、军事医学、维和行动和扫雷等领域分别成立了专家组开展合作。东盟与有关国家还多次举行上述领域的联合演习，可见其在推动安全合作方面持有强烈的意愿和动力。“ADMM +”的设立标志着东盟在地区安全领域既实现了与各大国的安全合作与关系平衡，又初步构建了以其为中

① 魏玲：《关系平衡、东盟中心与地区秩序演进》，《世界经济与政治》2017 年第 7 期，第 58 页。

② 《第四次东盟防长扩大会在菲律宾举行》，中国新闻网，2017 年 10 月 24 日，http：//www.chinanews.com/gj/2017/10 - 24/8359708.shtml。

心的安全合作网络体系。

其次，EAMF 是聚焦于海洋安全这一主题，由政府官员和专家学者参与的 1.5 轨多边对话合作机制。在 2015 年蓝图中，东盟致力于设立东盟海事论坛（AMF），并将该论坛打造成为东亚各国开展海洋安全合作的重要机制。2010 年 8 月，印度尼西亚主办了第 1 次 AMF。在 2011 年 11 月的 EAS 上，经日本提议，决定与之前的“ADMM +”同样，以 AMF 为基础，纳入对话伙伴国，设立 EAMF。2012 年 10 月，在菲律宾举行了首次 EAMF。目前，EAMF 已经发展成为就开展海洋安全合作以及相关问题进行交流的重要合作机制，在促进亚太国家海上合作、政治互信等方面发挥了重要作用。EAMF 在东盟主导下，避免了利益相关国无谓的争论，有效地保持着本地区海域的安全与稳定。[①] 东盟通过集体行动，能够在一定程度上保障东盟的共识和规范在更大范围内得以适用，这一过程也确定了东盟在地区安全框架中的中心地位。东盟一方面拉拢大国来弥补自身在地区安全治理上的不足，另一方面在大国间维持巧妙的平衡，使东盟在地区安全形势中处于更加有利的位置。[②]

在各种多边合作机制中保持中心性的同时，东盟与大国的

---

① 韦红、卫季：《东盟海上安全合作机制：路径、特征及困境分析》，《战略决策研究》2017 年第 5 期，第 36 页。

② 周玉渊：《东南亚地区海事安全合作的国际化：东盟海事论坛的角色》，《外交评论》2014 年第 6 期，第 142 页。

双边关系也取得了诸多进展。《东盟宪章》规定有东盟协调者制度，“成员国作为协调者，应当轮流在与对话伙伴国关系上全面负责协调和发展东盟的利益”。在其框架下，东盟国家作为协调者，与对话伙伴国结对，相互协作来维护东盟的利益。早在《东盟宪章》生效前，东盟国家与大国就存在结对帮扶的“惯例”，而东盟协调者制度就是对该“惯例”的制度化认可。这种结对每三年更换一次。例如，日本在 2012 ~ 2015 年与柬埔寨结对，在 2016 ~ 2018 年与文莱结对。2015 ~ 2018 年，越南担任东盟 - 印度关系协调者，与印度明确了 26 项优先合作领域的行动计划，并于 2018 年 1 月促成印度主办东盟与印度建立对话关系 25 周年峰会。[①] 此外，2015 ~ 2018 年，老挝与俄罗斯结对。但与其他对话伙伴国相比，俄罗斯与东盟国家的关系相对疏远，加之俄罗斯正遭受西方制裁，难以提供有力帮扶。

同时，东盟对话伙伴国在印尼雅加达设立常驻代表处，并派遣驻东盟大使。以 2010 年美国在雅加达设立常驻代表处为开

---

① 〔越〕《越南在担任东盟—印度关系协调员国任期内留下了深刻印记》，越南之声广播电台，2018 年 1 月 27 日，http：//vovworld. vn/zh - CN/新闻/越南在担任东盟印度关系协调员国任期内留下了深刻印记 - 614986. vov。〔越〕《阮春福出席东盟—印度纪念峰会：越南为东盟与印度关系发挥协调作用》，越通社，2018 年 1 月 22 日，https：//zh. vietnamplus. vn/阮春福出席东盟印度纪念峰会越南为东盟与印度关系发挥协调作用/75755. vnp。

端，目前已有中国、日本、澳大利亚、新西兰、韩国和印度等对话伙伴国在雅加达设有常驻代表处。各国驻东盟大使与东盟秘书处保持日常联系和沟通，不断加强本国与东盟的合作关系，同时也承担 EAS、“10 +3”、ARF 等多边会议的准备工作。这反映出各大国重视对东盟外交，也从一个侧面体现了东盟的中心性。

四　东盟多边外交战略的特点

如前所述，打造“开放性共同体”这一支柱在 2015 年蓝图中已有规划，2025 年蓝图只不过是对既有规划的继承。但对 2025 年蓝图和 2015 年蓝图进行比较之后可以发现，升级后的东盟多边外交战略具有如下特点。

第一，进一步加强与大国的合作关系，有效提升东盟所主导的多边合作机制的地位。值得注意的是，“开放性共同体”的行动计划强调要增强东盟主导机制的有效性，加强和对话伙伴国以及其他大国的合作。在其他支柱中，东盟也强调加强与大国关系和东盟主导合作机制的重要性。例如，在 2025 年蓝图中，第二个支柱“在和平、安全、稳定的地区中建设具有活力的共同体”占了相当篇幅，从加强东盟的能力建设和东盟共同体的角度出发，特别强调 ARF、EAS、“10 + 3”、“ADMM + ” 等多边合作机制的重要性。

第二，加快实施非传统安全、核不扩散、海洋安全以及南海问题等涉及东盟国家共同利益的行动计划。上述行动计划既涉及东盟各国间合作，也包含和大国合作以及充分利用东盟中心性的多边合作机制。具体而言，东盟在灾害管理和应对紧急情况时应发挥主导作用，加强和对话伙伴国以及联合国的合作以解决跨境犯罪，提升 ARF 在增进政治互信和开展预防外交方面的重要性，在 ARF 和“ADMM +”等框架内开展联合演习，通过增强东盟中心性及其主导作用以推动海洋安全合作等。[①] 当然，东盟主导合作机制的作用在 2015 年蓝图中也有提及，而 2025 年蓝图则涵盖了 2015 年蓝图尚未涉及的“ADMM +”、海洋安全、EAMF 等新机制，进一步强调东盟主导多边合作机制的重要性。

第三，进一步加强和其他地区组织和机制间的合作，特别是与上海合作组织、南亚区域合作联盟、海湾合作组织、太平洋联盟、拉美共同体等多边合作机制的合作。对此，2015 年蓝图中也提及各机制间的合作，2025 年蓝图基本遵循了这一方针。但将这一点与增强东盟在全球化进程中的影响力融合在一起可知，加强各机制间的合作被放在更加重要的位置上。在第三个支柱中，东盟将合作的大国范围扩大至对话伙伴国以

---

① ASEAN, *ASEAN 2025: Forging Ahead Together*, Jakarta: ASEAN Secretariat, 2015.

外。在第二个支柱中，东盟强调要促进东盟国家参加联合国维和行动，积极参与以联合国为代表的国际行动。据此可知，东盟提倡在国际社会中增强其作用，这反映出东盟国家试图扩大其在全球事务中的影响力、提升其地位。

第四，高度重视海洋安全，合作项目更为多样和详细。特别是关于南海问题，2015 年蓝图虽然强调应完全履行《南海各方行为宣言》和尽早制定“南海行为准则”，但 2025 年蓝图对于该问题的规定更为详细和具体，这在一定程度上反映了南海问题的紧迫性。其中的行动计划包括完全履行中国和东盟在 2002 年签署的《南海各方行为宣言》、尽快制定具有法律约束力的“南海行为准则”，根据《联合国海洋法公约》等国际规则和平解决领土争端，确保基于《联合国海洋法公约》的航行自由等。上述内容在东盟领导人会议和东盟外长会议发表的联合声明或主席声明中均不同程度地得到强调，这超越了单个东盟国家的立场，成为东盟针对南海问题的统一立场。关于海洋合作，除了前述通过 AMF 扩大与各国的对话与合作来维持东盟自身的中心性以外，东盟还强调要与对话伙伴国进一步加强合作。

第五，特别强调要“加强东盟和中国之间的信赖关系”。这种把中国专门列入行动计划的做法，值得关注。与远隔重洋的美国相比，地处亚洲的中国地缘政治经济地位优越，东盟对美国是否具有继续在亚太地区扮演重要角色的意识和能力心存疑虑。加之中国与东盟国家政治互信关系不断提升，经济关系日益密切，东盟自然要探索与中国的共存之道。[1] 当然，东盟加强对华关系，并非等于抛弃美国那样的零和博弈。据此认为菲律宾、马来西亚或泰国等国“对华倾斜”的看法值得商榷。东盟国家在经济援助、安全等领域不断增进对华合作关系是不争的事实，但合作领域却是有选择的，在和中国保持沟通和协调的同时并非照单全收，也有异议和抵制。在和中国加强战略合作伙伴关系的同时，东盟国家和美国、日本、印度等国家也在加强双边和多边关系。

第六，东盟在实施多边外交战略过程中力图维护的“中心性”体现在其定期主办各级别多边会议以及相关文件中。通常情况下，前述各类多边会议大多与东盟外长会议或东盟峰会同期举行，且按惯例自动在东盟轮值主席国召开。同理，ARF 或 EAS 的主席自然由东盟轮值主席国担任，会议议程也由东盟轮值主席国主导。这从制度上保证了东盟的“中心性”。东盟在各类多边会议的议题设定和共同声明、主席声明的内容调整等方面也发挥着主导作用，特别是在部长级会议以下的技术官员层面的协调方面表现尤为突出。

---

① Bilahari Kausikan, “Dodging and Hedging in Southeast Asia,” *The American Interest*, Vol. 12, No. 5, January 12, 2017.

五　东盟多边外交战略面临的挑战

在构建东盟三大共同体过程中，东盟能否通过实施多边外交战略来增强其中心性和整体性，继而在国际社会中提升其影响力和地位，面临着以下挑战。

一是在中美等大国之间摇摆导致东盟的中心性和整体性受损。自进入21世纪以来，随着中国崛起，从美国奥巴马政府实施的“亚太再平衡”战略到特朗普政府提倡的“印太战略”构想，以及日本在政治和安全领域实施“自由与繁荣之弧”“俯瞰地球仪外交”等战略，大国之间的合纵连横愈演愈烈，东盟对此深感忧虑。不可否认，特朗普政府的东南亚政策具有短期性和不可持续性，东盟担忧美国把东南亚作为防止中国和平崛起和维护美国霸权的一个支点，这将在一定程度上损害东盟力图维持的中心性和整体性。

二是内部协调不一致导致东盟的相对边缘化。自东盟成员国扩大为10国以后，东盟国家间动机完全一致日益困难，各国将本国利益和东盟整体利益融为一体的动机减弱。例如，作为东盟领头羊和东盟国家中唯一的G20成员，印尼独自开展大国外交，东盟在其外交战略中的重要程度相对下降。在苏西诺执政时期，印尼较为关心跨越东盟的单边外交。佐科总统上台后，这一趋势更为明显。印尼总统外交政策顾问利扎尔·苏克马明确表示，东盟在印尼对外关系中曾经是“唯一的支柱”，但现在只是“支柱之一”。[①] 2015 年 6 月，印尼倡议和中国、日本、印度组成“亚洲四大支柱”，以推动“泛印度太平洋”的合作。由于印尼在东盟内部具有重要影响力，印尼等东盟国家优先本国利益的考量在一定程度上影响了东盟的整体性。此外，东盟国家处于不同的经济发展阶段，对于经济自由化的立场不同，这也是导致东盟相对边缘化的一个要素。与东盟 10 国均参与 RCEP 谈判相比，新加坡和马来西亚、文莱、越南 4 个东盟国家宣布加入日本主导的新版 TPP——《跨太平洋伙伴全面进展协定》（CPTPP），东盟担心会影响自身的向心力和整体性。[②]

三是东盟多边外交战略存在一些自相矛盾之处。近年来，亚太地区大国竞争加剧，东盟自身既有的组织运行机制无法适应激烈变化的国际关系。东盟对于加强和大国的合作以及通过以其为中心的合作机制进一步促进东盟三大共同体建设的认识，和保证东盟中心性的认识互为表里。换言之，东盟只是中小国家集团，与大国相比，其领导力和影响力相对弱小。但尽管如此，东盟通过大国的相互牵制和其对东盟的照顾，从机制上保持了在亚太地区一体化进程中的中心性。当然，东盟国家

① Poole Avery, “Is Jokowi Turning his Back on the ASEAN?”, *The Diplomat*, 7 September, 2015.

② 毕世鸿：《RCEP：东盟主导东亚地区经济合作的战略选择》，《亚太经济》2013 年第 5 期，第 22 页。

如何在确保独立自主的同时，能够在贸易、投资、金融、市场对接、援助、基础设施建设等领域，把大国的力量和资源充分用于本国的经济社会发展，也是一个重要的课题。不容忽视的是，进一步加强和大国的合作，以及借助东盟主导的多边合作机制来推动东盟一体化进程的考量，却有可能动摇东盟的内部团结，并降低东盟自身的影响力。近年来，东盟在其一系列官方文件中一再强调要维护自身的中心性，也从一个侧面反映出其抱有的危机感，担心东盟不能长期保持对于地区事务的影响力。

四是东盟通过实施多边外交战略所形成的制度性或习惯性多边合作机制，并不确保东盟能够自动且长期维持其“中心性”。为了应对这一挑战，促使中美日印等国认识到参加以东盟为中心的多边合作机制的有效性，且能够切实持续参加这些机制，东盟必须按照2010年3月东盟峰会主席声明强调的那样，在内外两方面做出努力。对于一体化发展和共同体建设等内部课题，东盟要采取各种措施，通过维持和增强东盟共同体的凝聚力，不断说服各大国认识并承认东盟在多边合作机制中作为一极的重要性。在对外关系特别是对大国关系方面，东盟应彰显域外国家参加以东盟为中心的多边合作机制的有用性，特别是东盟主导的多边合作机制能够有效解决域外国家间的双边或多边问题。[①]

① Chin Kin Wah, “ASEAN's Centrality in the EAS,” *Southeast Asia - New Zealand Dialogue: Towards a Closer Relationship*, Singapore: ISEAS, 2007, pp. 42 - 44.

结　论

在亚太地区，中国崛起和中美博弈已成既定事实。但亚太地区国际关系的特点也在于，任何大国均无法无力在本地区建立或维持其霸权。东盟国家难以单独抗拒大国的压力，而东盟作为地区组织就发挥了不可替代的中介作用。东盟积极实施多边外交战略，显示了对大国政治发挥影响的意志和能力，但东盟主导成立的多边合作机制难以突破大国竞争关系也是不争的事实。东盟能起的最佳作用，就是防止大国博弈演变成对抗，继而颠覆东南亚的和平与稳定，更不希望出现任何一个大国独霸地区事务的格局。[①] 东盟的多边外交战略无疑面临诸多挑战，但东盟国家的多边外交战略因时而动，对于在各大国间保持距离、贸易和经济自由化等重要问题采取各自的因应之策。在存在上述多样性的前提下，东盟国家又能维护东盟的整体性并有效应对大国和维持其中心性，可谓东盟发展过程中一个值得持续关注的课题。

今后一段时期，大国间竞合关系并存，不会出现迫使冷战期间东盟国家选边站队的困境。各大国都在采取不同的方式争

① 〔新加坡〕《社论：亚细安必须坚持和平主导与团结》，《联合早报》2018 年 2 月 9 日。

取东盟的支持，对于东盟维持其在亚太多边合作机制中的中心性表示理解，给予一定程度的宽容和配合。在大国间没有发生军事对抗或激烈对峙的情况下，东盟不会分裂。东盟在多边外交中采取多极平衡和多头下注策略，极力避免卷入大国竞争的漩涡。这使得任何大国都难以在东盟对外关系中占据突出的影响力，继而获取大国的合作与支持，以此来扩大东盟外交空间，并实现自身利益最大化。对于各大国而言，让东盟在上述双边和多边合作机制中发挥引导作用，在东盟主导的合作机制中展开良性竞争，从而维持亚太地区的合作关系和稳定秩序，也是利大于弊。

当然，在亚太地区既有的多边合作机制中，也并非都以东盟为中心。东盟在 2025 年蓝图中提及要和上海合作组织、南亚区域合作联盟等加强联系与合作，从而在各个领域和层面来确保自身的存在感。对于东盟而言，如何以集体的名义彰显“东盟的中心性”并非愿景而是实态，至关重要。就东盟多边外交战略而言，东盟国家能够在多大程度上以东盟的名义做出贡献值得关注。对于东盟国家而言，东盟这一地区组织成功应对大国权力转移的基石乃是“遵守国际社会共通的原则和规范”，即国际社会共同的原则和规范对于其维系在国际社会中的生存和发展至关重要。东盟国家在对“大国主导国际关系”这一事实烂熟于心的同时，也在充分发挥自身潜在影响力的能动性。如果东盟国家能够超越国家利益的藩篱，基于大国平衡并采取共同措施，即便无力解决大国间的纷争，也能在一定程度上防止大国间紧张关系的升级，对过渡期的亚太地区国际关系起到稳定阀的作用。东盟和东盟国家的这种尝试，对于亚太地区所有国家而言，也是一种有益的借鉴。

新型国际关系与新型周边关系

Greater Mekong Sub - Region (GMS) and China Cooperation: Current Situation and Prospects for a New Type of Neighboring Relations

Nguyen Duy Loi *

1. Introduction

The Greater Mekong Subregion① (GMS) is a geographic

* Nguyen Duy Loi is a reseacher of Institute of World Economics and Politics, Vietnam Academy of Social Scienccs. Deputy Editor - in - Chief, Review of World Economic and Political Issuese.

① The Greater Mekong Subregion Cooperation initiative was proposed by Japan and the Asian Development Bank in 1992.

area with an area of 2. 6 million km^2 and a total population of 333. 8 million, including countries and territories located in the basin of the Mekong: Vietnam, Cambodia, Laos, Myanmar, Thailand and Yunnan Province and Guangxi Province of China. This is the expansion of the Greater Mekong Subregion, which do have 2 Chinese provinces. Cooperation in the GMS aims at promoting and facilitating mutually beneficial economic development among countries, bringing the Greater Mekong subregion rapidly expanding into a rapidly growing and prosperous Southeast Asian region.

With a length of more than 4800 km, the Mekong is the longest river in Southeast Asia and the 12th largest river in the world. The Mekong sub-region is flooded by the Mekong River and the tropical climate is favorable; The Mekong sub-region is particularly strong in terms of agricultural production and is the largest paddy granary in the world; economic structure shifted towards industrialization and modernization; Economic growth in this area is also impressive. A young, dynamic population structure, the Greater Mekong subregion has a great potential for human resources and a potential consumer market.

The GMS has a unique geographic location, bridging links with major markets and dynamic Asian economies such as China,

India and ASEAN. With such advantages, the Greater Mekong Subregion has the potential to become the center of production-consumption of ASEAN and an important link in the global value chain; It serves as a bridge for traffic, trade and investment among East Asian countries. With the development potential of this subregion, many partners are interested in cooperation, while the Mekong sub-region has also formed many cooperation mechanisms within the Mekong region as well as between the Mekong countries and the Major players such as USA, Japan, China, EU, Korea and India. With geopolitical and geo-economic potential and advantages, the Mekong countries can become a dynamic economic sector that serves as a driving force in the development of Southeast Asia.

Trade relations and investment between the GMS and China are growing rapidly, pushing their interdependence growing. The GMS sees opportunities to access the Chinese market as a lump of 1.3 billion people with a rapidly rising average income; increased trade, investment and ODA from China. On the contrary, China wants through GMS cooperation to promote Yunnan and Guangxi provinces of China to expand market, increase investment, increase labor mobility in the sub-region, compete with Japan and US, taking the leading position of economic integration in East

Asia. An equally important factor that the GMS countries attract China is rich natural resources to meet the demand for raw materials, fuel for Chines production. China has launched a "one axis, two wings" foreign strategy in which the GMS countries have been selected as an inland wing in this strategy. Moreover, the Chinese government also launched the "Belt and Road Initiative" (BRI) —a framework for the China's multi-national economic development through two component plans, on the mainland, the Economic "Belt of the Silk Road" and the 21st century Maritime Silk Road on the Sea. The initiative focuses on connectivity and cooperation between Eurasian countries, primarily the People's Republic of China (PRC). "On this basis, China has decided to increase its participation in cooperative activities in the GMS."

2. Overview of GMS Cooperation Relations with China

2.1 Infrastructure development cooperation

In the last five years, China has been one of the partners contributing to the development of the transport infrastructure in the Greater Mekong Subregion. By promoting infrastructure cooperation in the GMS, China wants to play a greater role in geo-economic, geopolitical and geo-strategic changes in the region.

The GMS is interconnected through three main channels: (i) The Mekong River originates from Tibet, China; (ii) economic corridors; and (iii) cultural and social links. Since 1992, the GMS countries have worked together on investment programs in various fields. There are all six priority areas, including: (1) Transportation, (2) Telecommunications, (3) Energy, (4) Human Resources, (5) Environment, (6) Investment; in 1994, GMS added Tourism; in 1998, trade and investment were divided into two independent sectors; in 2001, agriculture was also classified as a priority investment.

At present, the improvement of the transport infrastructure system is the most important because it creates a network linking the border and inland transportation infrastructure, thereby reducing transport costs and promoting export and import export. The 10th Mekong Transport Conference (STF 10), held from 21 - 23 March 2006 in Vientiane, the GMS countries agreed on several major initiatives, including Transport Sector Study (TSS). Subsequently, the GMS countries have implemented several TSS-based transport projects, for the period 2006 - 2015.

At the fourth summit meeting in Nay Pyi Taw, Myanmar in December 2011, the GMS countries set up the Regional

Investment Framework (RIF) within the framework of the new Strategic Framework for the 2012 - 2022 GMS. RIF includes transport-related projects to expand and develop GMS economic corridors, multi-disciplinary approaches, and multi-media projects. During the period 2014 - 2018, GMS invested in transportation, accounting for 90.2% of total investment in nine priority sectors. Investment trends in transport infrastructure will continue to be maintained and developed until 2020.

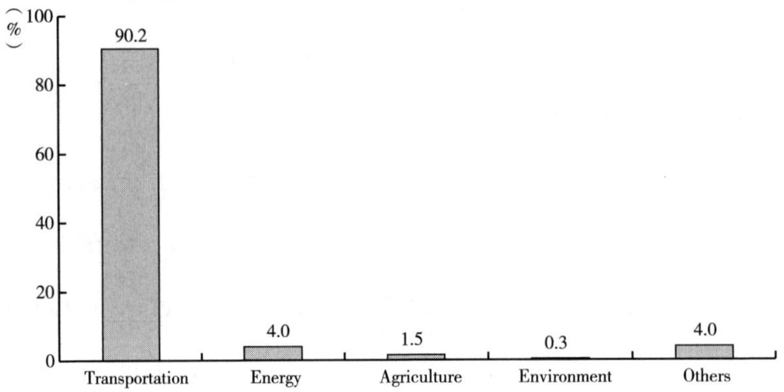

Figure: Regional Investment Framework 2014 - 2018

Sources: ADB 2016

China is one of the participating GMS partners through three coordinating agencies, the State Development and Reform Commission, the Ministry of Foreign Affairs and the Ministry of Finance. The main objective of China's participation in GMS cooperation is expressed in three main points: i) connecting corridors between southwestern China (Yunnan Province) and Indochina Peninsula; ii) connect southwestern China and Southeast Asia; iii) promoting economic relations, exchanges, enhancing economic, technical and scientific cooperation at various levels, in various forms and in many areas. In addition, the GMS cooperation aims to establish mutually beneficial economic relations, build the appropriate international investment and trade environment, build long-term and friendly relations of friendship and stability between China and other countries in the GMS and ASEAN.

Since 1992, China has made great efforts to connect Yunnan province (2004 to Guangxi) with the GMS countries. Yunnan province, located in the southwestern border of China, lies deep in the inland border with Laos, Myanmar and Vietnam in the west and south, has a 4060 km-long border and is close to Thailand, Cambodia, Bangladesh and India. Owning its rich natural resources and geographical advantages to Southeast Asia, Yunnan remains poor and underdeveloped.

In order to build Yunnan province into a large urban, green economy developed, China determined to actively promote the development of GMS cooperation. Yunnan province is part of the

Greater Mekong Subregion（GMS）Cooperation Program：（i）Yunnan province is located in the upstream of the Lancang-Mekong River, which flows through Yunnan Province, which is 1247 km long. Geographically, Yunnan province is in the Mekong River Valley. This is of course Yunnan province join the GMS.（ii）Yunnan province needs to expand exchanges with Southeast Asia and South Asia. To change backwardness, Yunnan province needs to build a transport network linking Southeast Asia, leaving the closed transportation model and opening up to the sea. The GMS program, which builds three North-South transportation corridors, is only to connect Yunnan province, southwest China with GMS countries. As the starting point of the three North-South transport corridors, Yunnan province played an important role in building this transport corridor, including the economic corridor.（iii）The fact that Yunnan province is more and more open to the outside world has really benefited. Participation in GMS Cooperation, Yunnan province may have more convenient exchanges with the world market, strengthening complementary economies of ASEAN. Thus, Yunnan province is fully capable of utilizing all resources and markets at home and abroad to promote economic and social development.（iv）Maintain a peaceful environment.

2.2 Trade and investment between the GMS and China

Since the establishment of the China – ASEAN Free Trade Area (ACFTA), trade between China and other GMS countries has been growing faster, with GMS increasingly becoming a major player in China's trade. Transactions between China and Laos and Myanmar are concentrated in Yunnan province. Yunnan's GDP increased sharply from $ 33 billion in 2000 to $ 160 billion in 2012, and double in 2016 by boosting cross-border trade. Kunming city has become an important and major focus of economic activities, attracting the participation of countries in the region such as Laos, Myanmar, Vietnam and many other countries. China's infrastructure investment strategy has made Yunnan province a focus area with the interference of most of the roads, railways, telecommunications, and power lines. This area is supported by the manufacturing division from the neighboring cities of Yunnan and Guangxi provinces. It then conducts production and trade policies with the GMS countries.

China has invested in many joint ventures or Chinese businesses joining economic and trade cooperation zones in Cambodia, Thailand and Vietnam. The Chinese government has established a National Research Coordination Group for the Development of the Greater Mekong Subregion in 1994. In addition to the proposed projects, China has also spent $ 30 million constructing the Kunming-Bang

Kok Expressway running through Laos, \$ 5 million for the improvement of maritime navigation in the upper Mekong region; 20 million yuan to study the feasibility of building a rail line linking the eastern part of Singapore with Kunming city. During the investment and development of transport infrastructure at GMS, China attaches great importance to the "Forward to the Southwest" strategy in order to develop Yunnan and Guangxi provinces.

The GMS economies have attracted FDI from their three partner economies in ASEAN, including China, Japan, and Korea, in recent years, because of their low cost of production and growth, fast economic and abundant natural resources. China is one of the dominant investors in some CLMV countries. In Cambodia, Chinese companies have become the largest producers, accounting for 50 percent of FDI in manufacturing, textiles and apparel. In Laos and Myanmar, China has invested heavily in infrastructure projects. Japan and Korea are also active investors in manufacturing, real estate and finance. Korean investors have rapidly expanded their investment in CLMV, especially with Samsung's investment in Thai Nguyen, so recent FDI flows have helped the CLMV economies. China's direct investment in Cambodia, though largely focused on garments, began to diversify into light manufacturing industries such as electronics and bicycles, thus increasing diversity in export products. In Laos, FDI into hydropower still accounts for a large proportion of total FDI. However, these countries need to attract more selective FDI, focusing on green, high-tech and friendly environment FDI from China, etc..

Table: Share of FDI by 3 partner countries and ASEAN in CLMV, % of total FDI

Host				
Cambodia	China	22.5	32.1	31.6
	Japan	3.0	4.9	3.1
	S. Korea	14.0	6.2	4.2
	ASEAN5	19.1	11.2	14.9
Laos	China	35.1	67.3	61.6
	Japan	0.4	0.2	7.0
	S. Korea	2.5	1.4	4.2
	ASEAN5	4.7	11.8	7.6
Myanmar	China	30.2	7.5	1.9
	Japan	1.4	4.0	3.4
	S. Korea	0.0	1.2	1.3
	ASEAN5	44.6	69.8	74.5
Vietnam	China	10.7	2.3	3.2
	Japan	26.6	10.5	8.1
	S. Korea	19.9	35.3	29.6
	ASEAN5	23.0	16.4	17.6

ASEAN5 consists of Indonesia, Malaysia, Philippines, Singapore, and Thailand.
Nguồn: ASEAN stats.

Through cooperation, China could exploit its resources to develop Yunnan and Guangxi provinces; Yunnan is the commercial bridge linking southwestern China with the interior of Southeast Asia, South Asia. The establishment of inland trade will reduce dependence on navigation in the South China Sea and the Malacca Strait. China has agreed with Myanmar to build a pipeline from the Bay of Bengal to China, which will allow China to receive oil from vessels from North Africa, or the Middle East, for a shorter period of time, reduced cost; In the event of a war, the Malacca Strait is halted, the supply of energy to China will not be interrupted.

At the first GMS Greater Mekong Sub-region Summit in 2016, China promised to provide GMS partners with preferential loans worth more than $ 11.5 billion, of which USD 5 billion will be allocated to specific projects on energy cooperation in the Mekong River Basin. There are five Chinese power plants operating in the area, and two are under construction in China and Laos. As expected, in the near future, at least 10 hydro power plants will be built—6 in Laos and 4 in Cambodia. It seems that China intends to continue to develop energy cooperation with its neighbors in the Greater Mekong subregion to mitigate the arbitrary problem of taking water from the largest river in the Southeast region.

2.3 Collaboration in addressing traditional and non-traditional security issues

There is still a dispute over territorial sovereignty and EEZ under the 1982 UN Convention on the Law of the Sea between some countries in the GMS and China. Sovereignty claims in overlapping waters are not clearly defined. If not peacefully dealt with under the 1982 UN Convention on the Law of the Sea between the countries concerned, there may be a risk of conflict, including armed conflicts between the countries involved.

Many other non-traditional security issues have not been properly coordinated and handled by GMS and China, such as food security, environmental pollution control, water pollution, epidemics, drug trafficking, and Transnational crime, The issue of sharing of water resource usage in GMS, China is subject to much criticism of the GMS for not paying adequate attention.

3. Prospects for a New Type of Neighboring Relations between the GMS Countries and China Cooperation

The 19th Communist Party Congress ended in October 2017, shaping China's development policy in the next five years and marking China's development strategy by 2050. After the 19th Congress, China's external relations are not only important for China but also affect regional and international politics. In the full text of the political report of the inauguration of the 19th Congress of the

Chinese Communist Party, presented by General Secretary Xi Jinping, attached to the theme of the Congress was "... determined to complete the success of a comprehensive social development. The Great Victory of Socialism with Chinese Characteristics in the New Age, Tireless Efforts for China's Great Renaissance Dream"① .

After the 19th Congress, the prospects for the Greater Mekong subregion relations with China will be further advanced. Promoting cooperation with GMS, China has economic, social and strategic advantages, particularly in Yunnan and Guangxi provinces, which are inland China and undeveloped economies in the eastern provinces.

Transport infrastructure is an important factor promoting trade and attracting foreign direct investment. In the GMS, Thailand has a synchronous transport infrastructure system, which is currently being developed in Vietnam, Laos, Myanmar and Cambodia, making it an attractive new investment destination in the region. China can cooperate in building and the development of a transport infrastructure system (road and rail) deep in the continent that is more accessible to seaports thanks to the transport infrastructure,

① From http: //vov. vn/the – gioi/ho – so/nhan – dien – trung – quoc – qua – bao – cao – chinh – tri – trinh – bay – tai – dai – hoi – 19 – 687472. vov.

contributing to the regional production networks will accelerate the movement, geo-economic shift in favor of countries located deep in the continent. In the GMS relationship with China, it seems that the two sides are mutually beneficial, except that they have not cooperated together to effectively exploit water resources in the Mekong River, as China does not join the Mekong River Commission (MRC). Joining the GMS and ASEAN cooperation, China hopes the strategy of exploring the West will be faster and more effective, while increasing its role in the region. Therefore, the Mekong region is a very important area for China.

The 9th Mekong Economic Corridor Forum, held on 22 September, 1977, in Vietnam, the ministers expressed strong support for the new GMS Transport Strategy, To build a seamless, efficient, reliable and sustainable GMS transport system. This goal will be achieved by improving links with South Asia and other places in Southeast Asia, promoting cross-border traffic, enhancing inter-modal connectivity and developing delivery and receive logistics services, while improving road traffic safety.

The cooperation deals with traditional and non-traditional security issues. Regard to traditional security issues, at present, there are three regions that have sovereignty over the exclusive economic zone in the GMS: i) territorial sovereignty and economic privileges in the East Sea (South China Sea); ii) exclusive economic zone in the Gulf of Thailand: between Vietnam, Thailand and Cambodia; iii) Andaman Sea, between Thailand and Myanmar. China may play a greater role and responsibility in addressing these issues.

Regard to non-traditional security issues, water resources sharing and environmental security issues in the Mekong River. To ease the tension in the sharing of water resources in the sub-region, China, for the first time in its history, agreed to provide full information on the regime ahead of the Sanya summit. operating hydropower plants. In the past, China kept this data secret and considered it a strategic information. The issue of environmental security in the Mekong River is one of the key issues that have a great impact on GMS cooperation. However, over-exploitation, over-exploitation, weaknesses in the management of the Mekong River in each country, lack of comprehensive and accountable cooperation among the countries in the sub-region are a problem. There are other non-traditional security issues that GMS can cooperate with China, such as food security, water pollution control, disease control, drug trafficking and transnational crime, etc..

The 9th GMS Regional Economic Corridor Forum was held on 22 September, 1977 in Vietnam, GMS Ministers approved the GMS

Regional Investment Framework 2022 (RIF 2022), through a list of 222 investment and technical assistance projects worth $ 64 billion. This entire list is intended to support the Hanoi Plan of Action. This is a list to call for support from the development partners and private sector to help the GMS countries complete national priority programs and projects in the period 2018 – 2022.

The GSM Partnership Program is driven by the three C: connectivity, competitiveness and community. These are the areas where China can cooperate to play a more important role through the Bank for Infrastructure Development (AIIB) and the "two corridors one belt", "one belt one road"; etc..

It is possible to enhance the GMS cooperation with China through the GMS 2016 – 2025 Tourism Strategy to facilitate the development of more competitive, balanced and sustainable destinations; Establishment of the Mekong Tourism Coordination Office as an intergovernmental organization; promote safe and environmentally friendly agricultural products; Strengthening the integration into the value chain.

In addition, GMS and China may enhance cooperation on: (1) trade facilitation; (2) Public – Private Partnership to enhance GMS trade and investment; (3) human resources training to improve competitiveness. /.

References

ADB (2017), GMS Ministerial Conference, Truy cập trang web: https://www.adb.org/countries/gms/greater-mekong-subregion-gms-conferences.

Heinrich Böll Stiftung, WWF and the International Institute for Sustainable Development (2008), *Rethinking investments in Natural resources: China's emerging role in the Mekong regio*n, Policy Brief.

https://www.adb.org/documents/adb-annual-report-2016.

http://vov.vn/the-gioi/ho-so/nhan-dien-trung-quoc-qua-bao-cao-chinh-tri-trinh-bay-tai-dai-hoi-19 - 687472. vov.

Nguyen Duy Loi (2017). The main economic challenge of some countries in the Greater Mekong Subregion. Review of World Economic and Political Isues, No. 8 (256), in Vietnamese.

Nguyễn Duy Lợi (2017). Prospects for the Mekong subregion cooperation relations with China after the 19th Congress, *APEC workshop report*, held in Hanoi on 18/11/2017, in Vietnamese.

Lu Guangsheng (2016), *China seeks to improve Mekong sub - region cooperation: Causes and policies*, *Policy Report*, Nanyang Technological University.

Nathanial Matthews and Stew Motta (2015), Chinese State - Owned Enterprise Investment in Mekong Hydropower: Political and Economic Drivers and Their Implications across the Water, Energy, Food Nexus, *Water*, Volume 7, 6269 - 6284.

The Greater Mekong Subregion Economic Cooperation Program (2017), *Statistics on growth, energy, and bilateral trade in the Greater Mekong Subregion* (Third Edition), truy câp trang web: https://www.greatermekong.org/sites/default/files/gms - statistics - 3rd - ed - view - pdf www.aseanstats.org/.

Xiangming Chen and Curtis Stone (2013b), *How China and Southeast Asia are reshaping the Mekong region*, East Asia Forum.

Xiangming Chen và Curtis Stone (2013a), China and Southeast Asia:

Unbalanced Development in the Greater Mekong Subregion, *The European Financial Review*, August - September 2013.

Yos Santasombat (2015), *Impact of China's rise on Mekong region*, Social Science Publisher.

Zhu Zhenming (2010), Mekong Development and China's (Yunnan) Participation in the Greater Mekong Subregion Cooperation, *Ritsumeikan International Affairs* Vol. 8, pp. 1 - 16 (2010).

中美战略博弈与中国周边军事合作

张　芳*

摘　要： 周边国际军事合作始终是中国军事外交布局的重点。然而，近年来，从奥巴马政府时期的“亚太再平衡战略”到特朗普政府的“印太战略”，以及美国已然执行的对华大战略都深刻地影响着亚太地缘政治格局，美国一贯的“零和博弈”战略思维和对中国周边国家的军事关系的运作都对中国周边军事合作产生着影响。这个世界上不变的只有变化本身。危与机相伴相随，形与势因人而变，斗与合辩证统一，而体现其间的奇正之道则考验着我们应对战略博弈的中国智慧。

关键词： 军事关系　中美战略博弈　中国周边军事关系

* 张芳，国防大学政治学院副教授，主要研究方向为军事战略、军事外交、中美军事关系。

一直以来，周边国际军事合作始终是我国军事外交布局的重点。中国坚持与邻为善、以邻为伴，倡导并践行共同、综合、合作、可持续的亚洲安全观，探讨构建平等、互信、包容、共赢的安全合作架构，深耕细植与周边国家军事关系，坚持因国施策，通过高层交往、深化联演联训、人员培训、能力建设等军事外交模式，不断丰富中国与周边国家军事外交的内涵和外延。总体上，我周边国际军事合作呈现高层交往深化战略互信，对话磋商突出安全关切，人员培训厚植文脉影响，联演联训拉紧安全纽带的特点。

然而，近些年来，从奥巴马政府时期的“亚太再平衡战略”到特朗普政府的“印太战略”，以及美国已然执行的对华大战略都深刻地影响着亚太地缘政治格局，美国一贯的“零和博弈”战略思维和对中国周边国家的军事关系的运作都对中国周边军事合作产生着影响。

一 美国对华大战略

近年来，随着美国战略焦虑感的不断攀升，特朗普政府通过《国家安全战略报告》、《美国国防战略》及新版《核态势报告》，赋予了未来对华关系以“长期战略竞争”的主色调，且将这种战略竞争几乎覆盖了所有的领域。美国国防部发布的《中国的军事力量与发展态势报告》和特朗普于2018年8月

13 日签署的 2019 财年国防授权法案，则欲将中国“战略竞争者”角色进一步固化，不仅要求美国防长就中国在太平洋和印度洋地区的军事行动定期向国会相关委员会做出报告，还要求将报告内容告知美国在亚洲地区的盟国和伙伴国，同时以合适的方式公开。这一法案成为落实特朗普政府提出的所谓“自由开放的印太地区”概念的具体推进措施。

应当清醒地认识到，美国战略具有持续性和稳定性的显著特点，美国对华战略的调整并非一朝一夕之役，而是自 20 世纪末以来美各方力量持续已久的战略研判和评估的结果。美国新安全战略表达出的世界观和总基调对中美关系产生了直接的不良影响。至此，美对华战略调整动作已经完成，可以预见的是未来很长时期这一战略主基调不会发生轻易调整，对美抱任何的幻想都无异于与虎谋皮。

早在 2013 年，美国的智库、战略家们就要求美国政府修订对华大战略，核心理念是调集美国一切实力，以保持东亚的主导地位。智库们分析认为，21 世纪，只有俄罗斯、未来的中国，还有潜在的日本才拥有扩张的基础：它们共同的特点是可以在一年以内的时间里承受一场常规战争，与世界上最强大的国家进行一场作战；同时，这个国家不仅要有令人生畏的常规力量，还要有能够承受其他国家核打击的核威慑力量。

二 美国的战略运作对中国周边安全的影响

美国对中国的发展形势的研判每天都在进行，而美国对中国实质性战略遏制早在特朗普政府宣布对华战略竞争之前就已然开始运作。这些战略运作对中国周边安全的影响不言而喻，主要表现在以下几个方面。

其一，美国战略重心持续东移引发地区动荡。美国试图通过海上围堵把中国塑造为亚太公敌，通过对地区安全的反设计引发地区性的军备竞赛，制造地区安全上的“囚徒困境”，引起地缘板块的动荡，由此进一步控制日本和东盟，刺激东海和南海的冲突相互震荡。其具体军事部署集中表现为美军日益强化在太平洋的三线部署态势。

一是优化驻日、韩美军前沿配置，扩大东南亚军事存在，提升一线应急作战能力。美国从 2012 年开始实行亚太再平衡战略以来，其在西太平洋的东亚战略部署就在发生变化。第一岛链，即从日本到菲律宾到琉球群岛再到新加坡。八年前美国在日本驻军有约 5 万人，韩国近 3 万人。但到 2015 年，美国租用了菲律宾的四个空军基地、一个陆军基地。美国在新加坡设置的联合后勤支援中心同样给美国的导弹驱逐舰和濒海战斗舰提供补给支持。这些基地和补给形式为美国在南海提供了一种现实的军事存在，使其不仅控制了南海的南端，而且控制了马六甲海峡的东端。

二是扩建关岛基地，打造战略枢纽，提升二线力量投送能力。美军的二线部署主要是指从关岛到澳大利亚的弧形地带。目前，关岛已被美军打造成美国干预亚太的重要基地。以其轰炸机部署来看，2016 年 8 月，美国首次在关岛同时部署现役三种主力轰炸机。今年年初，美军太平洋司令部实施“轰炸机持久存在”行动，再次出现三种战略轰炸机齐集亚太的罕见局面，意在确保美国对地区局势的掌控，让盟友放心，表示其可为盟友提供可靠的战略力量平台。美国在全球范畴内移动轰炸机不仅影响到其地区盟友，更影响到太平洋地区的联盟结构。达尔文港是澳大利亚通往东南亚及南海的门户，地处交通要冲，且军事设施相对完善，海军驻泊条件和基地面积得天独厚。2010 年之前，作为美国盟友的澳大利亚从未让美军驻军，但自 2011 年起情况发生变化——美澳达成为期 25 年的军事协议，美国使用达尔文港对海军陆战队进行轮训。尽管 2017 年初，美国总统特朗普在与澳大利亚总理特恩布尔通电话时，对奥巴马执政时期与澳大利亚达成的难民接收承诺大发雷霆，并直接挂断电话，引发美澳外交风波，此外 2017 年 1 月 30 日特朗普退出 TPP 的决定，也让澳大利亚深感不满，但这些并没有影响美澳军事协作的深化。据美国广播公司新闻网 2 月 12 日报道，部署在达尔文港的美国海军陆战队员在接下来数年将会翻倍，到2020年之前将会达到2500人。①

三是建设夏威夷和阿拉斯加的联合基地，部署后备力量，提升三线立体支援能力。依照“平时广域分散、战时快速集中”的“弹性聚合”理念，美军提出到2020年，将海军力量的60%、海外空军力量的60%部署到亚太地区，将太平洋舰队所辖部队的60%部署到东亚/西太平洋地区。美军最终的计划是把11艘航母中的6艘，73艘核动力潜艇中的42艘，以及空军海外力量的60%，包括全部185架F-22型战斗机中的1/3都部署到亚太地区。西太平洋地区已经出现第三舰队与第七舰队“双舰队”共存的局面。

其二，美国密织印太地区的军事关系网络。通过“2+2”对话机制巩固地区联盟体系，将日本打造成太平洋地区的干预中心，在亚太安全事务中充当“北锚”，自2006年以来日美加强以“西南诸岛”作战为背景的各项军事训练与演习，提高部队夺岛作战能力；让澳大利亚充当“南锚”角色；在韩国部署“萨德”，无限期推迟战时作战指挥；与泰国通过“金色眼镜蛇”演习令其发挥更大作用；美在新加坡外海部署濒海战斗舰，新加坡为美提供樟宜海军基地。据不完全统计，仅美海军太平洋舰队在亚洲地区每年就有上百场军事演习，这还

① 杨一帆、单珊：《美澳政治疏离军事紧密：F-22进入达尔文港，继续重返亚太》，澎湃防务-澎湃新闻，http://www.thepaper.cn/newsDetail_ forward_ 1618952，最后访问日期：2018年6月2日。

不包括阿拉斯加“北方红旗”、朝鲜半岛的“关键决心”等军演。其中仅第七舰队和陆战队举办或参加的就有125场，而美海军全球军事演习总共不到200场，其中一半以上都在亚太，足以见其对亚太的重视程度；另外，超过90%都是跨国演习，除了跟常见的日、韩等盟友的，就是拉拢其他东南亚国家的，这既是美军熟悉亚洲战场的过程，也是加深这些国家了解的程度；从演习的协同级别上来看（美海军把海上多国演习由浅到深分为5个级别），目前美军与孟加拉国、文莱、柬埔寨、印尼、马来西亚、菲律宾、新加坡、泰国、东帝汶等国的军事演习达到2级，跟印度等国家的军演达到3级，跟新澳泰菲等盟友/准盟友则达到4级，与日韩等则达到5级。2019财年国防授权法案对加强亚太地区部分国家的军事关系做了一系列安排，包括美国国务院将对斯里兰卡提供3900万美元的“对外军事资助”，以强化其保卫海洋安全的能力。7月30日，蓬佩奥在出席美国商会组织的首届印太商业论坛时高调宣称将“向印太地区的技术、能源及基础设施项目投资1.13亿美元”。8月4日，美国国务卿蓬佩奥在新加坡又宣布，将向印太地区追加3亿美元安全投资，帮助地区国家强化防务能力。

其三，一些地区国家不断加码与美军事合作力度。美不断加码与印太地区部分国家军事合作力度有美国战略上的主动，但也不乏地区国家深刻的双边根源和内在的驱动因素。一种是通过联合军演等方式提升军事合作密切度，譬如，美日联合军演已经向着美日南海联合外交与安全战略方向发展。另一种是通过达成防务协议，促进军事合作机制化。美印先后签署了《美印防务合作框架协议》和《后勤保障协议》，美承诺帮助印度发展航母弹射技术和飞机发动机，允许使用对方的军事基地进行补给，此前，只有美国的盟国才可以互相使用军事基地进行补给。与特朗普提出的“印太”概念相呼应，2018 年 5 月 31 日，美军宣布将“太平洋司令部”更名为“印太司令部”，此前，印度还曾借主办“瑞辛纳对话会”之机，促进美、澳、日、印四国形成潜在的对华统一战线，复兴 QUAD 的概念。近年来，美越军事合作不断升温，2018 年，美航空母舰在 1975 年越南战争结束 43 年后首度造访越南岘港。此前，2016 年美越签署了 2018 ~ 2020 年阶段防务合作行动计划，并于当年宣布全面取消对越南的武器出口限制；2017 年，越南国家主席陈大光出访美国，成为特朗普上台之后第一位正式到访白宫的外国元首。

三　中国的战略选择：变与不变

这个世界上不变的只有变化本身。危与机相伴相随，形与势因人而变，斗与合辩证统一，而体现其间的奇正之道则考验着我们应对战略博弈的中国智慧。

（一）变化的形与势

“强弱，形也。”“勇怯，势也。”自2018年初以来，美军在南海问题频频挑衅，不但派出军舰和轰炸机多次在南海执行所谓的“航行自由”以及“飞越自由”等行动，更每每辅之以美国军方高官的威胁言论煽风点火，使南海问题成为中美安全领域难题中的焦点。

5月，美军单方面宣布收回早前发给中国参与2018年“环太”军演的邀请，理由是与军演的原则和目标不符。2018年8月13日签署的2019财年国防授权法案更有多处直接涉及中国的条款，反映了特朗普政府对华政策取向。首先，该法案不仅要求美国防长就中国在太平洋和印度洋地区的军事行动定期向国会相关委员会做出报告，还要求将报告内容告知美国在亚洲地区的盟国和伙伴国，同时以合适的方式公开。此外，2019财年国防授权法案还特别提到南海，要求美国防长的报告应包括中国在南海的任何活动，包括陆域吹填、防御部署以及基础设施建设等，并禁止其邀请中国参加“环太平洋”多边军演。值得注意的是，为了给媒体提供更多素材，时隔3年后，美军开始用军机搭载CNN记者抵近中国南海岛礁海域。CNN随后公开在机上近距离拍摄的中国岛礁的影像资料。其次，强化对台军事交流是该法案的另一重要内容。该法案明确要求五角大楼加强与台湾地区的防务关系，帮助中国台湾地区提升其军事力量，其中包括支持中国台湾地区通过对外军事销售制度、直接的商业销售等获得现代化武器，并加强美国与台湾地区高级别官员的“直接交流”。7 月 7 日，美国海军两艘宙斯盾级导弹驱逐舰由南向北穿越台湾海峡。7 月 8 日，美国太平洋舰队公开证实这一消息。尽管其表示这只是“例行性移动”，但近年来美舰以往穿越台湾海峡的行动，美方并未如此高调证实并宣扬。

（二）不变的理念：建构亚洲命运共同体

亚洲命运共同体昭示着亚洲是亚洲人的亚洲，亚洲的安全需要亚洲人自己共同维护；基于对地区公共安全产品的共同需求，与周边国家的国际军事合作是地区性公共安全产品的重要平台。美国通过特朗普政府新国家安全战略报告得以向世人展示了他们眼中这个充满丛林法则、零和博弈和权力争夺的世界。在奥巴马的“亚太再平衡”战略基础之上，特朗普将美国带到距离中美两个大国合作机会窗口更远的地方。有学者曾经指出，今天的中美又站在了世纪的十字路口。此话差矣：又站在十字路口的是美国，而非中国。此前的历史中，中国是无以选择的，因而无所谓十字路口；而今天的中国是因为坚定地秉承“人类命运共同体”理念沿着和平发展的道路向前挺进，因而也无所谓十字路口。在今天美国抛弃其在立国之时曾提出的价值观外交之时，中国以“人类命运共同体”理念进行价值观外交可谓是正当其时。

一是冷静判断，清醒认知美国及其战略目的。客观评价美国，要避免夸大美国的衰落，避免低估美国的国际领导力和对美国未来趋势的错误判断。对于美国国家实力我们需要一个理性全面的认知和判断，不能过高估计，但也不能低估。高估美国我们的国家利益会受损，低估美国国家实力和意志力的人，动辄鼓吹对抗性的对美安全战略也必将误导中国领导人，使中国国家利益付出代价。同时，也要看到美国自身所具有的强大的自我修复能力。美国一直有其两面性：消极的一面和发展的一面。就经济成长而言，除了爆发金融危机的2008年，美国新世纪以来仍在逐年增长，它的经济规模在过去15年中提升了75%，其增量大约相当于四年前我国的全部经济产出。当今世界具有这样全球投送能力的只有美国。不清醒地认识到美国的韧性，就无法理解当前世界的复杂。

美国借由“印太战略”实现对亚太地区经济整合进程的反设计——实现“制造并维持可控的紧张”——利用亚太地区缺少安全框架的设计，制造矛盾争端，阻断亚洲的合作进程，同时也阻断这一地区的经济整合进程。一方面，美国通过在印太地区的投兵布阵，渲染中国威胁论，增加中国周边对中国的安全压力，继而加强军备建设，跟美国走；而周边增加军备的举动和跟美国走的态势反过来又使中国感受到了威胁压力，中国不得不增加军备。无论是中国周边国家加大对军备的投入还是中国自身加大对军备的投入，都无形中会在加强国防投入的同时减少经济建设的投入，这实际上会迟滞中国经济的发展。可以说，美国渲染中国威胁论，在亚太地区推行过去的“亚太再平衡”战略和现在的“印太”战略可谓是一石二鸟。美国战略东移的态势将是一个长期趋势。

中国威胁论的实质是通过渲染威胁来制造紧张，通过制造可控紧张阻遏中国的发展。中国致力于围绕“命运共同体”这一理念建构互利共赢的新型国际关系，中国始终是世界和平的建设者、全球发展的贡献者、国际秩序的维护者。中国作为全球经济的主要贡献者，为世界经济安全做出的贡献有目共睹，如今，特朗普政府又为“中国威胁论”提供了一个新的翻版，但却更加不得人心。正如王毅外长所指出的：“因为事实胜于雄辩。中国是全球经济增长的主要贡献者，年均贡献率达到30%以上，超过了美国、日本以及欧元区国家的总和；中国是全球减贫事业的主要贡献者，贡献率超过了70%，创造了人类历史上的奇迹；中国还是维护世界和平的主要贡献者，我们成为联合国安理会五个常任理事国当中派出维和人员最多的国家，维和经费出资居世界第二位。此外，在过去五年中，中国还通过提出共建‘一带一路’等重大倡议，成为参与全球治理、维护贸易自由化和开放型世界经济的主要贡献者。”①

二是传播世界一流军队的价值理念，提升军事影响力。习近平主席在党的十九大报告中擘画了到21世纪中叶把人民军队全面建成世界一流军队的战略蓝图，这一战略目标同样引领着我军以先进的外交理念探索区域性军事合作模式的步伐。什么是世界一流军队？世界上是否曾经有过世界一流军队？从硬实力上来说，世界一流军队未必是世界实力第一的军队，但应具有维护国家领土安全和主权完整的能力，具有慑强敌于第二岛链之外的区域拒止和反进入能力，具有相应的保护海外国家利益的能力。从软实力上看，世界一流军队拥有引领世界爱好和平国家的国际观、和平观、安全观以及由此而积淀出的深厚的道义感召力，从这个意义上来看，世界一流军队并非只是单纯强调军事实力强大，它必须有着努力带着爱好和平的人们走出丛林法则、零和博弈的强大理念、行动影响和责任担当，有着超越单边主义、霸权行径，堪为世界各支优秀军队表率的一流的优良作风。在此基础上，才能开世界军事合作模式之先河创造性地推进中国与周边国家军事合作。对此，当前在建构世界一流军队的外部形象塑造上还需要缩小亚洲命运共同体和对外阐释的距离、缩小亚洲命运共同体与周边军事合作的距离、

① 《2018年全国“两会”期间外交部部长王毅就“中国外交政策和对外关系”回答中外记者提问》，新华网，http：//www. xinhuanet. com/politics/2018lh/zb/wzjzh/wzsl. htm。

缩小中国周边老朋友和新朋友之间理解程度的距离。这些都有赖于我方加强对周边国家军事历史、军队建设和军事文化的国别研究，并在此基础上打造融通中外的新概念、新范畴、新表述，讲好中国故事，提供中国方案；需要加强因国制宜的周边安全合作的策略研究，为中国承担地区安全责任，当好地区安全合作的推动者、公域安全的维护者和公共安全产品的提供者给予充分的理论支持。

国家间的博弈胜出与否，与军事影响力的升降、国际军事话语权的掌控本质相关。军事影响力是国家以安全战略意图为出发点运用其军事力量而产生的外部性反应，表现为不通过强力说服他国、使其顺从要求的能力。需要强调的是“不通过强力”，即不通过军事力量的战争运用而使他国顺从要求的能力。因此，排除了对外战争中的军事力量运用，将主要聚焦的是军事交往的方式。人类既往历史中曙光乍现的短暂和平岁月无一不在告诫人们：军事与政治内在而紧密地关联着——如果不愿意使用“最后手段”诉诸战争，就需要深入挖掘和最大化地运用军事影响力以保持和平。当前，我国特别需要让周边国家对中国有较为全面的认知，战略心理上具有确定性。无论是对当前我国的周边关系还是“一带一路”沿线国家间的合作关系都需要较长时期的深度经营。在“一带一路”倡议的推进中还需要我国努力实现硬实力与软实力的平衡，实现国际话语权与公共安全产品供给力的平衡。更多展示软实力，逐步消除部分邻国安全上靠美国的根基，从根本上改变“经济上靠中国，安全上靠美国”的局面。我国与美国的竞争，既是硬实力的竞争，更是软实力的竞争，当前更多地表现为对我邻国的争夺，对人心的争取。

话语权是指信息的传播力、影响力、公信力，既是力量，也是权力。同时，话语并非仅仅是话语，“话语就是语用”“话语就是实践”“话语就是通过论证达成共识”。提升我军国际话语权，是我们这支大国强军适应新时代内外形势要求的迫切需要，也是开展合作斗争、维护战略利益的重要手段，具有重大意义。首先，提升话语权就是“谋势”。从某种意义上讲，话语权也可以说是一种舆论态势的塑造力。这不是一兵一卒的运用，也不是一城一地的得失，而是一种战略态势的塑造，是一种谋势、用势、造势的战略能力。在与周边国家的军事合作中，我们行的是合作共赢的“王道”，而非零和博弈的“霸道”，需要通过提升国际话语权，广泛宣示中国特色的军事文化、军事战略、军事理论、军事行动，使周边国家明白我国防御性国防政策、积极防御的军事战略有着必然的历史逻辑，从而认同我国军事力量的建设和运用。其次，提升话语权其实是使中国军队声音走在中国军队前面，大踏步推动军事力量“走出去”。军队从来就是外向性的力量，一支不能走出国门、走向世界的军队很难成为世界一流军队。我军迈步走出去，拓展国家利益、维护世界和平、履行国际责任，迫切需要提升我军国际话语权，有序有效地传播中国军队好声音。与周边国家的军事合作是构建地区安全命运共同体的重要平台，中国军队承担着维护地区和平稳定、促进共同安全的使命任务，也迫切需要不断加强和提升话语权。最后，提升我军地区公共安全产品的价值感召力。近年来，我军在维护地区安全方面做出突出贡献，付出极大牺牲，提供了广泛公共安全产品，履行了大国责任。党的十九大报告明确提出，要不断增强意识形态领域主导权和话语权。这需要我们提升国际话语权，更积极有效地宣示我国恪守维护世界和平、促进共同发展的外交政策宗旨，宣示我们致力于推动建设相互尊重、公平正义、合作共赢的新型国际关系，宣示共同、综合、合作、可持续的新安全观，宣示我国防御性国防政策和积极防御军事战略方针，同时注重放大国家、责任、勇敢、奉献等世界各国军队共同的价值理念，对冲意识形态对抗声调，在交流、交锋中实现交融。

三是创新军事合作模式。作为世界性大国，中国复杂而独特的周边安全环境使其难以对地球上的任何一个大国处理周边安全关系进行学习和借鉴，中国成功处理周边安全问题本身就会成就一种研究范式——这是一种大国与小国之间的、非对称力量之间的安全合作模式。更何况因为各方都会参与到博弈与磨合当中，而这一地区又缺乏一个类似欧盟的地区机制，要形成全新的稳定的各方均能接受的关系将受多重因素的影响和考验。历史上，世界性大国崛起路径中的“胡萝卜加大棒”的美国模式，都违背了中国今天所倡导的命运共同体理念。中国所寻求的合作模式需要军事合作视域下的周边学研究超越传统的或军事结盟、军事对抗的思维模式，探索出一条经济上合作共赢、安全上互信团结、民心上相互融通的地区安全合作模式；在策略上坚持深耕内线与经营外线的统一，把握合与斗的辩证统一，保持主动有利的战略态势为地区命运共同体提供更多地区公共安全产品。

从对话平台建构的视角，以香格里拉峰会和香山论坛为例做进一步分析。2018 年 6 月，第十七届国际战略研究所（IISS）亚洲安全峰会（香格里拉对话会）在新加坡举行。中国人民解放军军事科学院副院长何雷中将率团参会。打造好中国自己的军事话语平台，这是建设世界一流军队的应有之义，也是中国持续推进国际军事合作，增强中国军队的国际话语权，为中国提供“麦克风”的关键要素。香山论坛影响力近年来的持续提升表明香山论坛与香格里拉对话会在未来极有可能形成亚太地区安全架构中的南北呼应态势。为此，需要持续精耕细作让中国特色的香山论坛引领世界性安全议题真正地“论”起来。因为，中国特色如果只有特色，不具有世界性就不具有解释性。香山论坛当然不能成为香格里拉对话会的翻版，只有超越香格里拉对话会才可能达到中国获得优势话语平台的目的。香格里拉对话会之所以能成为当前亚太地区规模最大、层级最高的非官方安全论坛，得益于其会议议题的开放性、组织的灵活性、内容的创新性和角色的多边性。譬如，从议题设置来看，17 次香格里拉对话会每年的议题不止一个，往往会有 3～5 个，但第一个议题往往是美国的防务政策或美国在亚太地区的安全角色，而其余的议题往往随地区热点问题而随机设置。譬如第 12 届有军事现代化与战略透明的议题，第 11 届设置了网络战的议题，而第 10 届则专门讨论了亚洲新的力量分布和意义的议题，甚至在第 8 届时也加入了波音公司的议题。显然，不只是安全议题，与安全相关的经济议题也是香格里拉对话会的内容之一。从参加角色来看，外交部长、国防部长、高级别安全官员、军队领导人等都是香格里拉对话会的主角，部分外交团体、企业领袖及学术界和媒体界人士也会出席对话会，而组织形式的灵活性则为他们提供了多场双边或三边会见，使各国关心的议题能够得到多个视角，进行充分的交流。我方在组织香山论坛时只有设置更为多元的议题，提出更多富有创建性的、可操作性的地区安全建议，提供更加多样灵活的讨论方式，让参与者有话想说、有话能说、有话尽说，确实感知到平台的吸引力和讨论的充分性，才能对香格里拉对话会有所超越。

总体来看，特朗普政府一方面加紧亚太布局，试图通过“印太战略”扩容战略控制半径，实现对亚太地区安全秩序的干涉；另一方面，特朗普政府又通过这一干涉本身制造“新中国威胁论”，加强与中国台湾的军事关系，破坏中美关系，借“印太战略”本身强化地区安全关系网络。这些都对奉行“地区命运共同体”的安全理念，积极推进、深化与周边国家的军事合作的中国带来一系列挑战。但对于外交理念明确，安全价值观广受认同，国家正面积极的国际形象逐渐丰满的中国，这亦不失为一个让中国对外战略不断成熟，以更加积极主动的态度去应对挑战，深度经营与中国周边国家军事合作的重要时机。

从培育期进入成长期的澜湄合作

澜湄国家命运共同体视角下的澜湄反恐合作机制构建

周洪旭*

摘　要： 澜湄机制下的政治－安全合作是对澜湄国家以往以经济合作为核心的区域合作模式的重要突破，但政治－安全合作进展不大的实际情况，某种程度上制约了澜湄合作的深入推进和澜湄国家命运共同体的构建。结合澜湄国家所面临的恐怖主义新形势，现有反恐合作中存在的问题及相关国家对进一步加强反恐合作的实际需求，本文认为澜湄反恐合作机制的构建是十分必要的且可成为当前推进澜湄合作之政治－安全合作的最佳切入点。我国应以此突破澜湄政治－安全合作的瓶颈制约，增进澜湄国家的政治互信，努力构建和平共处、相互尊重、合作共赢的政治安全关系，从而进

* 周洪旭，大理大学助教，云南大学国际关系研究院2015级博士研究生。

一步推动澜湄国家命运共同体的构建进程。

关键词： 澜湄合作　命运共同体　反恐机制

2015 年 11 月，中国和湄公河五国共同创立澜湄合作机制（以下简称“澜湄合作”），2016 年 3 月，中国和湄公河五国举行首次领导人会议，提出打造面向和平与繁荣的“澜湄国家命运共同体”。这是首个得到了相关国家正式认可、已经进入建设议程的命运共同体。澜湄合作机制从正式诞生至今两年有余，澜湄合作成效显著，充分体现了“澜湄速度”和“澜湄效率”。在深化澜湄合作的基础上，实现澜湄国家命运共同体的逐步成长，吸引和推动其他国家和地区更加积极地参与“一带一路”建设，是“一带一路”在东南亚取得成功的关键所在，也是当务之急。澜湄合作是政治 - 安全、经济、社会 - 文化合作“三位一体”的，纳入政治 - 安全合作是对以往以经济合作为核心的区域合作模式的重要突破。此外，政治 - 安全合作还对我国在澜湄次区域推进“一带一路”建设和构建周边战略依托有深远意义。同时应该看到，迄今为止澜湄合作框架下政治 - 安全合作进展不大，制约了澜湄合作的深入推进和澜湄国家命运共同体的构建。澜湄国家间存在的历史恩怨和现实竞争及对中国怀有畏惧、防范甚至“中国威胁论”的心理，影响了各方构建命运共同体的诚意和力度。[①] 澜湄次区域在传统安全和非传统安全方面的问题错综复杂地交织，给构建澜湄国家命运共同体带来了较大阻力。

近年来，随着国际恐怖主义形势的变化，尤其是“伊斯兰国”（Islamic State，以下简称 IS）中东战场溃败后的演变及发展，东南亚地区恐怖主义发展呈现出诸多新态势。东南亚地区反恐格局发生着深刻的演变，地区恐怖主义从海岛国家向半岛国家（湄公河国家）的北扩及蔓延，其中最突出的表现就是泰国和缅甸恐怖主义形势的急剧变化，老挝、越南及柬埔寨这些很少涉及恐怖主义问题的国家也凸显一些恐怖主义的苗头，我国境内新疆分裂主义极端分子通过我南部边疆进入东南亚的“南通道”，与东南亚地区整体恐怖主义北扩态势产生交汇、共振，导致澜湄国家边境沿线地区成为暴恐活动的潜在高危区。本文将结合澜湄国家所面临的恐怖主义新态势，分析澜湄国家当前反恐合作的现状及存在的问题，探讨构建澜湄反恐合作机制的必要性及推进路径。

一 澜湄国家面临的恐怖主义威胁

长期以来中国一直是恐怖主义的受害国，以“东突”为

① 卢光盛、别梦婕：《澜湄国家命运共同体：理想与现实之间》，《当代世界》2018 年第 1 期，第 42～45 页。

主的恐怖主义势力给中国的政治稳定、经济发展和民族团结造成了很大威胁。除中国外，其他澜湄国家近年来也面临着不同程度的恐怖主义威胁，并出现一些恐怖主义的新苗头。值得关注的是，澜湄国家所面临的恐怖主义威胁一定程度上受到全球恐怖主义形势变化及地区反恐格局演变的深刻影响。

（一）中国面临的恐怖主义威胁

随着国际恐怖主义形势的变化，当前中国面临的恐怖主义威胁主要来自以下几个方面。一是中国境内恐怖主义由新疆向其他内陆省份出现一定程度的扩散。二是在境外的中国公民、驻外机构不断遭受恐怖袭击。三是国际恐怖主义对中国国内安全稳定的潜在影响已升级。这种影响主要表现在国际恐怖势力对中国的关注越来越多和加入 IS 等国际恐怖组织的“圣战”分子的回流问题。四是中国周边包括南亚、中亚和东南亚在内的地区的恐怖主义形势不容乐观，尤其是东南亚地区近年来暴恐热点问题不断，这些地区的恐怖主义发展态势在中国周边形成环形恐怖主义包围之势。像 IS 和“基地组织”这样国际恐怖主义威胁中国周边地区及国家的内部稳定，最终使得中国在周边地区的利益存在及国内安全稳定所受的恐怖主义威胁不断增大。

（二）泰国面临的恐怖主义威胁

泰国国内面临的恐怖主义威胁主要集中在泰南四府（宋

卡府、也拉府、北大年府和那拉提瓦府），但近年泰国恐怖主义有朝泰国北部地区扩展并呈现出与“伊斯兰国”等恐怖势力相互联系的迹象。多年来，泰国政府出于维护国内政局稳定及国际旅游市场信心等多方考虑，一直未将泰国南部的分离运动与恐怖主义挂钩，当局更愿意称这些组织为叛乱组织，拒绝承认泰国南部分离势力与“伊斯兰国”等域外恐怖组织存在联系。然而近年来泰国的恐怖活动出现向中、北部扩散的态势，并给予“伊斯兰国”更多渗透空间。

（三）缅甸面临的恐怖主义威胁

近年来，由缅甸若开邦爆发进而蔓延扩大到缅甸其他地区的穆斯林群体与佛教徒群体的暴力冲突越来越严重。[①] 若开邦的“罗兴亚人”（另译作罗兴伽人）问题中出现涉恐因素，如2016 年 10 月“罗兴亚团结组织”（RSO）对缅甸边防警察局的袭击，是本地区第一次出现有 IS 背景的恐袭事件。缅甸“罗兴亚人”群体中的极端分子发动的暴力活动的模式发生转变，出现了“恐怖组织”的形式并主动向缅甸社会和缅甸政府/军方发动恐怖袭击，[②] 致使若开邦成为国际恐怖主义势力

① 郭继光：《缅甸政治转型过程中的宗教冲突探析》，《东南亚研究》2014 年第 6 期，第4 ~9 页。

② 伍庆祥：《“罗兴伽”的污名化——缅甸“罗兴伽”问题的文化过程》，《南洋问题研究》2018 年第 2 期，第 44 页。

试图积极介入的热点地区。若开邦的冲突局势和难民危机持续吸引着IS及“基地组织”“印度次大陆分支”的高度关注，中东、南亚和东南亚的恐怖组织大肆利用“罗兴亚人”受迫害的形象，并将受迫害的“罗兴亚人”叙事运用到对穆斯林群体进行极端思想宣传及招募的过程中。[①] 缅甸境内的“罗兴亚人”一直是IS意图拉拢的对象，IS曾表示要在孟加拉国建立一个基地，并以此为跳板向缅甸扩张其势力。[②] 不排除IS或其他恐怖组织进一步招募“罗兴亚人”极端分子的可能。曾在中东参战的IS成员也有可能将缅甸若开邦作为一个新的热点冲突地区，并将其作为开展恐怖活动的基地。随着超过百万“罗兴亚人”难民群体的向北扩散（主要是向西北进入孟加拉国及少量向东北进入我国）和滞留，涉恐风险也随之滋生。随着“伊斯兰国”对缅甸若开邦局势的关注和渗透，未来缅甸也有可能出现具有宗教极端主义背景的恐怖组织。

---

① Angelica Habulan, MuhTaufiqurrohman, Muhammad Haziq Bin Jani, Iftekharul Bashar, Fan Zhi'An and Nur Azlin Mohamed Yasin, "Southeast Asia Philippines, Indonesia, Malaysia, Myanmar, Thailand, Singapore, Online Extremism," pp. 17 – 18, *Counter Terrorist Trends and Analyses* (*CTTA*), Vol. 10, No. 1 (January 2018).

② Iftekharul Bashar, Counter Terrorist Trends and Analysis Vol. 7, No. 11 (January 2016), p. 25, http://www.rsis.edu.sg/wp-content/uploads/2014/07/CTTA-January-2016.pdf.

（四）越南、老挝、柬埔寨面临的恐怖主义威胁

越南、老挝和柬埔寨很少涉及恐怖主义问题，但近年也开始出现一些恐怖主义苗头，值得引起高度关注。2016 年 10 月 9 日，越南公安部首次正式公开认定，基地设在美国加利福尼亚州的“越南更新革命党”为恐怖组织。这是越南官方首次将“越南更新革命党”的恐怖组织定性向外界宣布。2017 年 12 月 28 日，越南官方对外宣布挫败了一起意图用汽油炸弹袭击胡志明市新山一国际机场的恐怖袭击，并逮捕了 15 名暴恐嫌疑人。①

近年来“占族哈里发”运动等新型恐怖势力在越南和柬埔寨的占族民众中的影响不断增加，越南部分占族出现涉恐倾向，“伊斯兰祈祷团”（Jemaah Islamiyah）对柬埔寨占族进行“泛伊斯兰极端主义”宣传。帕特里克·霍尔（Patrick Hall）指出，柬埔寨政府破获两名“伊斯兰祈祷团”头目为当地占族提供“泛伊斯兰极端主义教育”的案件，已经引起了国际社会的密切关注。② 中东瓦哈比学校资助柬埔寨占族穆斯林学

---

① “Vietnamese Court Sentences 15 For Roles in Airport Bombing Plot”, December 27, 2017, https://www.rfa.org/english/news/vietnam/vietnamese-court-sentences-15-for-roles-in-airport-bombing-plot-12272017161042.html.

② Patrick Hall, “Cambodia's Terrorists: Invoking Terrorism for Political Expediency”. *International Policy Digest*, 07 June, 2013.

校的资金也在增加，在柬埔寨超过400家清真寺是由外国基金支持修建的，占族穆斯林被宗教极端思想渗透的可能性不断加大。①

2016年1月24日以来，出现多起中国人在老挝遇袭事件。虽然不是所有袭击事件都涉及中国公民，但这样的事件接连发生在老挝这样一个较为和平稳定，且与中国长期保持友好关系的国家，不得不引起我们的关注与警惕。瑞士智库“指战员”（Offiziere）在题为《老挝的恐怖主义：缓慢的燃烧》的评论文章中指出，几十年来，老挝国内一直存在低烈度的叛乱，“老挝民族解放组织”（the Ethnic Liberation Organization of Laos）和“老挝解放阵线”（the United Front for the Liberation of Laos）这两个极端组织持续通过暴力手段以争取苗族少数民族的自治或独立。② 2012年联合国官员称老挝是极易受人口贩卖、毒品走私和有组织犯罪损害的国家，由于其易渗透的边界，常被恐怖分子当作中转站。③ 未来，老挝北部的分离势力可能与贩毒、武器走私和人口贩卖等有组织跨国犯罪集团的利

① Rohan Gunaratna&Stefanie Kam, *Handbook of Terrorism in the Asia - Pacific*, *Insurgency and Terrorism Series*: *Volume* 10, Imperial College Press, London, 2016, p. 138.

② Paul Pryce, “Terrorism in Laos: Slow Burn?”, August 21, 2016, https://www.offiziere.ch/?p=28723.

③ Rohan Gunaratna&Stefanie Kam, Handbook of Terrorism in the Asia-Pacific, Insurgency and Terrorism Series: Volume 10, Imperial College Press, London, 2016, p. 72.

益进一步交织，为恐怖主义在老挝的发展提供有利的土壤。

随着超过百万“罗兴亚人”难民群体的向北扩散（主要是向西北进入孟加拉国及少量向东北进入我国）和滞留，涉恐风险也随之滋生。东南亚的暴恐活动的“北扩”与新疆极端分子通过我国南部边疆进入东南亚的“南通道”会产生交汇、共振效应，导致我国和湄公河国家边境沿线地区成为暴恐活动的潜在高危区。

二 澜湄国家反恐合作现状

虽然没有专门的澜湄反恐合作机制，但澜湄国家分别从全球及东盟等（多边）层面、澜湄次区域（双边）层面开展反恐合作，也取得了一系列成果，对澜湄地区恐怖势力起到了一定的震慑作用。

（一）全球及东盟等（多边）层面的反恐合作

一是联合国层面的反恐合作。联合国是最有国际影响力和法定的最高层次反恐合作平台，中国一直倡导在联合国的平台下开展国际反恐合作。联合国于 2006 年 9 月 8 日通过了《联合国全球反恐战略》，也是澜湄国家进行反恐合作的重要指导。但就目前的情况看，联合国层面的反恐合作发挥的作用相对有限，联合国也鼓励各国家地区在遵循《联合国宪章》和

《联合国全球反恐战略》的原则下，积极开展地区多边及双边的反恐合作。

二是东盟机制下的澜湄国家反恐合作。东盟是打击地区恐怖主义的一个非常重要的平台，中国与东盟在非传统安全领域已经开展长期合作并取得一系列成果。东盟框架下的东盟地区论坛、东盟峰会、东亚峰会、东盟国防部长扩大会议、中国与东盟防务与安全对话、东盟－中国跨国犯罪部长级会议都是中国与东盟进行反恐合作的重要平台。

三是 APEC 机制下的澜湄国家反恐合作。中国、泰国和越南都是 APEC 的成员国，2015 年 11 月的 APEC 峰会打破了亚太经合组织（APEC）论坛的聚焦贸易和商业问题的惯例，呼吁各国加强反恐合作。会议形成的宣言称："经济增长、繁荣和机遇是根除恐怖主义和极端主义存在土壤的最有效措施之一。"①《亚太经合组织反恐和安全贸易战略》在加强国际合作反恐尤其是打击恐怖融资方面发挥着积极作用。2003 年成立的 APEC 反恐任务小组在协助成员识别和评估反恐需要、协助成员反恐能力建设、对成员反恐进行技术援助、配合相关国际和地区组织的反恐行动等方面开展了一些工作。2013 年 7 月，鉴于恐怖主义威胁的长期性，APEC 高官会决定将反恐任务小

① 《APEC 峰会宣言罕见提及反恐，呼吁加强反恐合作》，参考消息网，2015 年 11 月 20 日，http：//china. cankaoxiaoxi. com/bd/20151120/1003129. shtml，最后访问时间：2016 年 1 月 19 日。

组升级为反恐工作组。

四是亚洲相互协作与信任措施会议（简称“亚信会议”）机制下的澜湄国家反恐合作。亚信会议是亚洲重要的地区性安全对话与合作论坛之一，中国、泰国、越南、柬埔寨为成员国。自 2002 年起，反恐一直是亚信会议的重要议题，对澜湄国家的反恐合作有着积极的促进作用。

五是其他非官方的多边机制。亚太安全合作理事会、香格里拉对话会议、香山论坛等非官方多边机制，在推进澜湄国家反恐合作方面也起到了积极作用。在最新一届（第 17 届）香格里拉对话会上，恐怖主义成为与会各国防务官员高度关注的问题，各国防务官员与专家纷纷呼吁，要通过发展教育、加强网络监管、提升国民生活水平等方式合力围剿新形式的恐怖主义。①

（二）澜湄次区域（双边）层面的反恐合作

一是中老缅泰湄公河联合巡逻执法。中、老、缅、泰四国于 2011 年 10 月 31 日发表了《关于湄公河流域执法安全合作的联合声明》。迄今为止，四国执法部门已完成第 73 次联合巡逻执法任务。在中老缅泰湄公河联合巡逻执法行动框架下，

① 《综述：香格里拉对话会上官员呼唤全球反恐新思路》，新华网，2018 年 6 月 3 日，http：//www. xinhuanet. com/world/2018 – 06/03/c _ 1122930646. htm。

四个国家的执法部门一起开展湄公河联合巡逻执法，共同防范、打击和制止湄公河流域违法犯罪，共同应对突发事件，维护航运安全，对跨国犯罪起到了震慑作用。湄公河流域各种形式的跨国犯罪往往与恐怖主义活动密切相关，联合巡航执法活动为四国反恐合作奠定了一定基础。

二是中老缅泰柬越“平安航道”联合扫毒行动。2013 年，在中方积极倡导下，中老缅泰四国禁毒执法部门首次联合开展了第一届“平安航道”联合扫毒行动，2015 年邀请柬埔寨、越南两国加入并共同签订《“平安航道”联合扫毒行动三年规划(2016～2018)》。平安航道行动已上升为澜湄合作机制下一项重要的执法合作内容，有力打击遏制了湄公河流域毒品犯罪活动，维护了整个地区的安全稳定。2018 年六国已开始研究《中老缅泰柬越“平安航道”联合扫毒行动五年规划（2019～2023)》，探讨六国联合扫毒行动机制与澜沧江-湄公河综合执法安全合作中心的有机衔接。[①]

三是澜沧江-湄公河综合执法安全合作中心（简称“澜湄执法中心”）机制下的澜湄反恐合作。2017 年 12 月 28 日成立的“澜湄执法中心”是澜沧江-湄公河流域第一个综合性执法安全合作政府间国际组织，该中心将在尊重各成员国主权

---

① 《中老缅泰柬越 2018 年“平安航道”联合扫毒行动第二阶段总结会在景洪召开》，云南禁毒网，2018 年 8 月 28 日，http：//www.ynjd.org/PolLawWorks/BanNa/201808201167.shtml。

和法律的基础上，致力于统筹协调本地区预防、打击跨国违法犯罪，融合交流情报信息，开展专项治理联合行动，加强执法能力建设，为各成员国执法部门提供优质、高效的服务。

四是澜湄国家双边层面的反恐合作。2014 年中国和缅甸发表《中华人民共和国与缅甸联邦共和国关于深化两国全面战略合作的联合声明》，声明提到两国将加强在地区反恐、禁毒和打击跨国犯罪等领域合作，提高两国边境管理合作水平，及时就边境事务进行沟通，维护两国边境的安宁稳定。[①] 2018 年 2 月，中国反洗钱监测分析中心与缅甸金融情报中心签署反洗钱反恐融资金融情报交流合作谅解备忘录，中缅双方将基于互惠原则在涉嫌洗钱、恐怖融资及其他相关犯罪的信息收集、研判和互协查方面开展合作。[②] 2015 年 4 月 8 日，中国与越南发表联合公报，强调在反恐、禁毒、打击电信诈骗、出入境管理、边境管控、网络安全等领域合作。[③] 2015 年 7 月 30 日，

① 《中缅关于深化两国全面战略合作的联合声明（全文）》，新华网，2014 年 11 月 14 日，http：//www. chinanews. com/gn/2014/11 - 14/6777602. shtml。

② 《中国反洗钱监测分析中心与缅甸金融情报中心签署反洗钱反恐融资金融情报交流合作谅解备忘录》，中国反洗钱监测中心，2018 年 2 月 28 日，http：//www. camlmac. gov. cn/com/info. do? action = detail&id = 468。

③ 《中越联合公报（全文）》，新华网，2015 年 4 月 8 日，http：//news. xinhuanet. com/world/2015 - 04/08/c_ 1114906532. htm。

中越在中国河口成功举行“红河 1 号 -2015”联合反恐演练,[①] 为双方反恐合作积累了宝贵经验。中泰陆军特种部队反恐联合训练始于 2010 年，截至目前，双方已开展了四次反恐联合训练，对威胁当前全球安全的城市反恐作战中出现的新问题进行了卓有成效的训练。此外，2015 年中泰两国空军航空兵部队在泰国空军呵叻基地举行代号为“鹰击 -2015”的联合训练，中泰两军务实合作进一步深化。[②] 2016 年 9 月 13 日，中老首次联合反恐演练“云岭利剑—2016”在云南西双版纳州成功举行。中国云南西双版纳公安边防支队和老挝南塔省公安厅在演练中采取情报互通、联合指挥、联合封控、联合抓捕移交等警务合作机制，对暴恐分子实行联合打击。[③] 2018 年 3 月 12 日，中柬两国开启为期 17 天的“金龙 -2018”中柬两军反恐联合训练。主要展开反恐器材操作使用、轻武器实弹射击、徒手格斗、模拟机降、机动渗透和追捕搜剿等专业课目

① 《中越“红河 1 号 -2015”联合反恐演练在中国河口举行》，央广网，2015 年 7 月 30 日，http://news.cnr.cn/native/city/20150730/t20150730_519364385.shtml。

② 《中泰空军将首次举行联合训练，代号“鹰击 -2015”》，光明网，2015 年 11 月 11 日，http://mil.gmw.cn/2015-11/11/content_17690186.htm。

③ 《中老举行“云岭利剑—2016”联合反恐演练》，中国新闻网，2016 年 9 月 13 日，http://www.chinanews.com/gn/2016/09-13/8003186.shtml。

训练，旨在加强两军共同遂行反恐和人道主义救援任务的能力。①

三 澜湄国家命运共同体视角下的构建澜湄国家反恐合作机制的必要性分析

（一）政治－安全合作是当前澜湄合作及构建澜湄国家命运共同体的瓶颈因素

虽然中国与湄公河国家地缘相近、人文相亲、经济互补，建设命运共同体具备良好基础，但是，澜湄国家命运共同体建设仍处于关键的培育期，还面临一些推进障碍，② 政治－安全合作的深入推进也面临不小的阻力甚至成为澜湄合作的瓶颈因素。澜湄合作将政治－安全合作凸显出来，是我国同澜湄国家进一步加强政治互信，深化全方位合作的创新举措。政治－安全合作领域推进不畅，将极大削弱澜湄合作机制较其他次区域机制的相对优势，也制约着经济、社会－文化合作的实质开展。遗憾的是，目前澜湄合作的政治－安全合作进展不大，多停留在战略、愿景、规划层面。澜湄流域综合执法安全合作中心虽

① 《“金龙－2018”中柬两军反恐联合训练暨人道主义救援中方参演部队出征》，《解放军报》2018年3月14日第2版。

② 卢光盛、别梦婕：《澜湄国家命运共同体：理想与现实之间》，《当代世界》2018年第1期，第42～45页。

已成立，但在打击毒品走私、人口贩卖、跨国犯罪等非传统安全领域的合作还不够深入，且尚未有力突出反恐合作。澜湄国家先前参与的东盟框架内的或其他区域、次区域及双/多边政治－安全合作实效不大，且缺乏覆盖澜湄全部成员国的合作机制。次区域内安全公共产品严重欠缺，亟待澜湄各国做出更多努力。

（二）反恐合作是当前澜湄框架下政治－安全合作的最佳切入点

反恐符合次区域各国的共同利益诉求，易找到现实和紧迫的政治－安全合作契机。近年来，随着国际恐怖主义威胁的不断增大，澜湄次区域内各国面临的恐怖主义威胁呈上升趋势。新疆分离主义极端分子在澜湄国家的非法流动给地区安全带来诸多不稳定因素。虽然目前澜湄各国面临的恐怖主义威胁程度不同，可能出现对反恐的需求不对等，但当前形势下国际恐怖主义已呈现出全球性特点，从策划行动、人员招募、资金运作到打击目标尤其是软目标，都是全球性的，任何一个国家都不能在恐怖主义的威胁中独善其身。澜湄各国未来的反恐合作将转向更为积极的行动，从而找到现实和紧迫的政治－安全合作契机。

（三）构建澜湄反恐合作机制为澜湄国家间进一步加强政治互信提供现实意义

目前我国与部分湄公河国家如泰国、越南、老挝和柬埔寨开展了联合反恐演习，但规模仍然较小、覆盖面窄，尚未对恐怖主义起到震慑作用。澜湄国家缺乏反恐合作专门机制的顶层设计，反恐合作易受到各国政治因素影响而难以深入。构建澜湄反恐合作机制可以填补现有各类合作机制在反恐领域的相对缺失，也利于加强澜湄次区域国家间的政治互信，夯实澜湄国家政治-安全合作的基础。反恐领域的合作较传统安全的合作敏感性低，不会导致安全困境且易达到双赢甚至多赢的效果，可以成为次区域国家增强政治互信的一大砝码。

四 构建澜湄反恐合作机制的路径

一是加强政治互信，凝聚反恐共识。建议我国同其他澜湄五国一道充分考虑各国国情，尊重各方的核心利益，注重合作中的平等和信任，努力消弭各方疑虑与担忧，从注重务实合作、加强沟通、深入交流等角度入手，不断加强政治互信。强化打击恐怖主义的共同认识，摒弃“双重标准”，促进次区域内反恐安全合作共识凝聚。

二是借鉴上海合作组织和“中阿巴塔”等地区反恐合作机制的经验，创立符合澜湄国家国情及次区域需要的反恐合作机制。例如成立地区反恐怖机构，建立一套完整的反恐怖法律体系，定期召开反恐情报交流会，并建立反恐信息数据库。在反恐形势研判、线索核查、情报共享、反恐能力建设、反恐联合训练、人员培训方面，开展协调并提供相互支持等。

三是充分整合“澜沧江 - 湄公河综合执法安全合作中心”“中老缅泰湄公河联合执法”等现有执法安全机制涉及反恐合作的各项职能，争取反恐合作领域的早期收获。在现有执法安全合作机制的基础上，进一步深化打击跨国犯罪的合作，并拓展到打击恐怖主义的合作领域。在深化合作的基础上，争取反恐合作领域的早期收获，携手打造澜湄次区域反恐合作的新典范，并将合作的成果惠及澜湄所有成员国。

四是推动反恐合作协议谈判，早日签署反恐合作协议。建议可考虑由国家安全委员会领导，由外交、公安、安全等部门协调，以公安部国际合作局为主要牵头单位，推动我国同澜湄次区域国家的反恐合作协议谈判，争取早日签署澜湄联合反恐协议。可将澜湄国家间的反恐演习、反恐司法及警务合作等内容纳入反恐合作协议框架内，使其常态化、机制化。

五是设立反恐合作专门机构并将办事处落地边境省份，充分发挥边境省份在反恐合作中的前沿阵地作用。云南与湄公河流域国家一江相连，是我国最早参与“澜湄合作”的省份，未来可将云南省作为参与澜湄反恐合作的主体省份并赋予相应的权限，考虑设立“澜湄合作”反恐合作中心，并将中心办事处设在昆明市或景洪市。反恐合作中心具体协调澜湄国家间如情报交流与共享、反恐培训、反恐演练、边境管控、人员引渡等方面的合作。由此边境省份参与地区反恐的综合能力将得以提升，在反恐合作中的前沿阵地作用得以充分发挥，严防恐怖主义的触角伸到我国境内。

构建人类命运共同体是对恐怖主义进行全球治理的价值取向，各国应基于平等、公正原则，以实现人类命运共同体的总体利益为价值取向，寻求从根本上解决恐怖主义问题。[①] 构建澜湄国家命运共同体是澜湄合作的最终目标，澜湄国家命运共同体是人类命运共同体的先行先试样板，具有十分突出的探索和实践价值。澜湄次区域内恐怖主义问题日益突出，单个国家的反恐行动或双边的行动都难以应对复杂多变的国际恐怖主义形势及其对次区域带来的影响，更为深入的反恐合作将成为澜湄国家反恐战略的必然选择。

① 汪勇、梅建明:《人民日报人民要论：携手建构全球反恐战略体系》,《人民日报》2017 年 5 月 8 日第 7 版。

论大湄公河次区域环境安全复合体及其社会性建构

魏志江　詹雪琳*

摘　要： 大湄公河次区域环境安全复合体的形成，不仅仅由于其存在客观的环境安全威胁，也是由于体系层次的“全球环境认识共同体”和地区层次的国家，根据需要将本来属于公共问题性质的环境问题通过“安全化”建构为安全问题。这种安全化的过程，对次区域其他国家安全认知和实践产生了影响，次区域国家彼此间的环境“安全化”和“去安全化”过程已经不能分割开来解决。因而，在大湄公河次区域已经形成了环境安全相互依赖格局，从而形成了地区环境安全复合体。从环境安全复合体的极性来看，它形成了以中国为权

* 魏志江，中山大学国际关系学院教授兼副院长；詹雪琳，广州市零点调查公司环境问题研究员。

力中心，并成为大湄公河次区域环境安全复合体的一极，但由于其环境话语权上的缺失，大湄公河次区域环境安全复合体，并不是一个典型的中心化地区安全复合体，该复合体还存在东盟、日本、美国、澳大利亚等外来变量干预的权力关系。实际上，大湄公河次区域环境安全复合体是一个多边权力关系交织的结构。在社会性建构上，大湄公河次区域环境安全复合体基本形成了安全机制模式。相对良好的生存环境条件、相对温和的国家间关系、历史上建立的安全机制，使得大湄公河次区域在环境安全上得以避免冲突形态，并在安全机制的基础上呈现出向更深层次合作发展的趋向。

关键词： 地区安全复合体　大湄公河次区域　环境安全

自二战以来，湄公河流域的开发与合作，就一直是东南亚地区乃至世界的热点问题。在湄公河流域开发过程中的诸多安全问题中，环境安全成为该区域备受关注的重点问题。湄公河河流沿岸环境安全与否，关系着该地区的生存和可持续发展，由于环境问题的全球性和大湄公河次区域的重要战略地位，大湄公河次区域环境问题还集聚了联合国、东盟、美国、日本、环境非政府组织等邻近地区和域外势力的关注，因而该问题的影响力已经超越了本区域而具有全球性。近年来，对湄公河环境安全问题的研究，已经日益引起学术界的关注与重视。但是，毋庸讳言，目前的研究主要集中在围绕水资源引发的政治、安全问题和环境合作机制这两个主要关注点，缺乏从区域安全复合体的架构下，对湄公河次区域安全复合体进行整体性研究。由于大湄公河次区域对于中国经济发展和周边外交具有重要战略意义，因此，本文以区域安全复合体为研究框架，以探讨湄公河次区域的环境问题的安全化以及该复合体的内核结构和发展趋向。

一 大湄公河次区域环境的“安全化”与安全复合体的形成

根据巴里·布赞关于地区安全复合体的理论，形成区域安全复合体必须具有三方面的条件：首先一组单元要在地理上临近；其次至少要有一个行为体把某一或某些问题进行安全化，这种安全化过程相互交织进而在这一区域形成了安全相互依赖格局；最后这种安全上的相互依赖具有明显区别于其他地区的特征，使它们足以成为一个具有持久性特征的地区安全复合体。在地区安全复合体的形成中，“安全化”具有重要的作用。“安全化”是指安全化施动者声称某一安全指涉对象面临着“存在性威胁”，应通过打破常规的政治规则和政治结构来使这一公共问题上升到安全问题。[①] 安全化理论并不聚焦于某一问题是否客观上是威胁，而关注谁为什么、怎么样把这一威胁安全化？当某一样东西被称作安全问题时，安全化进程就已经开启了。简而言之，是“安全化”造就了安全问题。

当安全问题被提出来，即安全化进程开始之后，这种安全化行为对其他行为体的安全认知和实践产生了影响，这种安全化过程的相互交织，使行为体之间的安全问题已经不能分割开来解决，实际上这一区域已经形成了安全相互依赖格局，正是安全相互依赖格局，使这一区域的安全特征明显区别于别的区域，而使其成为地区安全复合体。即当一个地理区域内一群单元，形成了一种安全相互依存的格局时，安全复合体就出现了。所以地区安全复合体形成的中心环节是“安全化”。为考察这种安全化相互交织的过程，要弄清楚三个核心问题：哪个或哪些行为体，为什么要把这一问题安全化？它或它们是如何把这一问题安全化的？这种安全化行为对其他行为体的安全认知和实践产生了什么影响？

在环境领域，安全化步骤通常是从体系层次开始的。“全球环境认识共同体”能够敏锐地察觉到环境问题导因和结果

① 〔英〕巴里·布赞、〔丹〕奥利·维夫、〔丹〕D. 怀尔德：《新安全论》，朱宁译，浙江人民出版社，2003。

发生在哪一个层次，它们试图把导因和结果都安全化。“全球环境认识共同体”，通常包含与环境相关的国际组织、非政府组织、科学家和研究机构以及媒体，它们在全球层次，首先通过进行科学研究等相对权威的科学议程，对全球或某些地区的环境问题提出安全化动议。在这个过程中，也伴随着政治议程，比如在国际会议中就某一环境问题进行斡旋、发动公众进行群体活动、通过媒体影响公众舆论、对政府决策进行施压，等等。但在大多数情况下，环境问题安全化的政治议程，还是要由地方政府完成。因为主权国家拥有比国际组织和非政府组织更正式的权力。实际上在大湄公河次区域，环境问题的安全化也是由相关国际组织、非政府组织和研究机构、民间团体等“全球环境认识共同体”在国际上开启了这一问题的安全化，次区域国家再根据自己的需求实际完成了安全化。

对大湄公河次区域环境问题密切关注的国际组织有联合国环境规划署、联合国开发计划署、世界银行等政府间组织，与环境相关的非政府组织主要有拯救湄公河联盟、国际河流网络组织、世界野生动物保护学会、世界自然基金会等具有国际影响力的非政府组织以及一些有影响力的媒体。它们对大湄公河次区域环境问题的安全化步骤主要有以下几点。

首先，通过宣称经过科学论证，发现大湄公河次区域的相关环境问题存在“生存性威胁”，并主张通过采取紧急手段实现环境保护。联合国 2007 年发布的一份名为《大湄公河流域环境展望》的报告对湄公河流域的环境保护发出了警告，如果不对环境恶化做出回应，将导致无可挽回的生态破坏，也将增加贫困和农村人口所面临的健康威胁、自然灾害、食物匮乏和社会分裂等危险。[①]

其次，利用媒体引导公众舆论，通过调查民意、发动民众进行群体事件，通过“言语－行为”使公众相信次区域的环境问题确实存在“生存性威胁”。另外，利用“全球环境认识共同体”在国际上的影响力在国际会议、地区会议上进行斡旋，以影响政治议程。比如在1996年4月湄公河委员会和联合国开发计划署所举行的有关综合开发湄公河流域的研讨会就遭到了大多数非政府组织的抵制。体系层次上的“全球环境认识共同体”有关环境的安全化行为对次区域有关国家不仅造成了很大的舆论压力，在动员群众方面也给有关国家的政治稳定造成了一定的影响。因此，虽然国际组织和非政府组织缺乏主权国家的正式权力，但它们使得大湄公河次区域环境问题的安全化步骤在体系层面上是十分有效的。

虽然国际组织和非政府组织组成的“全球环境认识共同体”具有强大的资金和科研能力，并通过科学议程在全球层面上开始环境安全化的步骤，安全化的政治议程决定着安全化

① 陈世瑞：《大湄公河次区域环保合作——以莱茵河治理为借鉴》，《华南师范大学学报》2008年第28卷第5期，第69～74页。

最终完成的程度，而最终的完成程度还是要由地区层面所决定。不仅因为主权国家拥有着非国家行为体所没有的正式权力，而且对于一个地区来说，最重要的安全行为体是国家，最重要的影响因素是国家间关系。大湄公河次区域国家对环境问题的安全化举措有：首先，在国内官方的表述上把湄公河流域的环境问题上升为关乎国家生存与发展的安全问题。越南总理阮晋勇在 2011 年 12 月 14 日召开的第 27 次越南外交工作会议上强调，“对外工作的最高目标是置国家和民族的利益于首位，如相关国家在湄公河上游修建 11 座水坝电站，则下游的九龙江平原将会消失，当地民众将无法生存，这是正当利益，我们必须保卫”。[①] 其次，在发生湄公河环境问题纠纷时对其他国家可能对本国环境造成的威胁予以强烈的指责和威胁采取“紧急行动”。2000 年湄公河下游地区遭遇特大洪灾，下游国家政府和一些非政府组织把灾害原因的矛头指向中国，认为中国在湄公河上游的水坝建设导致了下游的洪灾。2010 年，湄公河流域遭遇了百年一遇的旱灾，下游国家和一些非政府组织又指责是中国建造的水坝导致下游水量减少才引发的旱灾。在当年的湄公河峰会上中国的水坝问题成为重点研讨的问题。除了对中国在湄公河上游建造的水坝可能造成的对流域生态环境

① 郭延军、任娜：《湄公河下游水资源开发与环境保护——各国政策取向与流域治理》，《世界经济与政治》2013 年第 7 期，第 136 ~ 160 页。

影响的担忧外，对沿岸其他国家可能对环境造成影响的行为也有不少的忧虑。比如本来打算 2010 年开始动工的老挝沙耶武里水坝就遭到了越南和柬埔寨的极力反对而不得不紧急叫停。柬埔寨的洞里萨湖是沿岸居民生活用水、渔业和水产养殖业的来源和基础，而沙耶武里水坝的建设可能会导致洞里萨湖水量减少，对居民的生产生活乃至柬埔寨的整个国民生计造成毁灭性打击。而水坝建设可能导致下游水量减少、引起湄公河三角洲海水倒灌，对越南也是不可接受的后果。泰国想要从湄公河引水的栖河－蒙河工程遭到环保人士和非政府组织的抵制，同时还遭到了下游国家柬埔寨和越南的反对。老挝甘蒙省纳凯高原的南通河 2 号水坝建设也引起了环保界的争议。

最后，与次区域的国家政府相对温和的安全化步骤相比，次区域的民间势力对环境问题的安全化影响也是剧烈的。组成“全球环境认识共同体”的不仅仅有体系层次的相关环境非政府组织和学术团体，还包括了大湄公河次区域的相关的民间组织。这些民间势力采取了与体系层次上的相似的环境安全化步骤。泰国《曼谷邮报》经常对中国在湄公河上游的行为可能导致下游的生态环境问题进行指责，甚至认为中国在威胁着湄公河的生存：“中国大坝扼杀湄公河”。[①] 安全化动议不仅需要

① 李承霖：《中国环境威胁论的传播特点及应对——以澜沧江－湄公河修建水坝舆论危机为例》，《对外传播》2016 年第 2 期，第 36～38 页。

施动者指认一个问题为安全问题，还需要听众接受它。而听众的这种接受不一定是主动的，可能是被动地接受这种话语的渲染或受到胁迫。这一步骤在大湄公河次区域比较容易完成，因为这一区域的许多地方实际上民众比政府有着更强烈的安全化动机。生态环境的破坏直接关系到很多民众的生产生活，他们对可能危害到他们生存环境的行为更加敏感。许多非政府组织利用这一点在民众中大肆开展关于环保的宣传，发动民众进行“反坝”等活动。经过政府和媒体的宣传，再加上自身的亲身体验，民众很容易就接受了“环境安全关乎我们的生存和生计”这个事实。

因此，大湄公河次区域环境问题安全化的程度，在不同的层次其实是不一样的。体系层次的“安全化”动议比较激进，而地区层次的政府“安全化”较温和，民间力量的“安全化”则较激烈。从“安全化”的政治效果来看，地区层次的“安全化”对于形成该地区的环境安全相互依赖格局的影响比体系层次要大。在体系层次上，由“全球环境认识共同体”所推动的安全化进程是相当有效的。全球层次的行为体由于强大的经济实力和国际影响力以及非政府组织相对自由的特征，能够剧烈地开展安全化步骤。在地区层次上，次区域除了中国以外的其他国家实力普遍比较弱小，在地区和全球上的话语权和行动能力都比较弱。这种相对弱小的国家状况，一方面使它们没有足够的能力把环境问题安全化，另一方面对其他国家在经济或能源方面的依赖，使它们在实施安全化的过程中不得不考虑这样做的后果。但由于影响地区安全的最重要的还是区域内的国家间的关系，因此即使次区域各个国家的政府对环境的安全化并不十分剧烈和彻底，但它的实施效果，却对地区安全态势有着决定性影响。因而虽然环境安全化在大湄公河次区域的国家间与主要由非政府组织主导的全球层次相比其剧烈程度要小得多，但由于国家行为体在地区层次的绝对影响力，地区层次安全化的实际政治影响力要超过全球层次的安全化步骤。因为即使次区域的环境安全化步骤，并不如世界上其他一些由河流联系起来的安全复合体那般剧烈（比如两河流域和尼罗河流域），但它仍然对各个行为体的安全认知和实践产生了深刻的影响和反应。比如在全球层次上，“全球环境认识共同体”对湄公河流域环境问题的关注给次区域各国都形成了压力，使它们不能不更多地关注次区域的环境问题以及重新审视本国的环境政策。在地区层次上，湄公河下游国家对中国在上游建造水坝可能造成的生态环境问题和对中国在上游控制水源的担心给中国造成了极大的压力，迫使中国不得不采取一定的措施来回应这样的质疑化解纠纷。在这种由内而生的环境威胁感知和外生的压力之下，次区域各国对环境问题的共同关注和实践，使它们逐渐形成了对于次区域环境安全一定程度上的共识，使它们之间形成了一种安全相互依存格局，这种相互依存格局最终导致了湄公河次区域环境安全复合体的形成（见图1）。

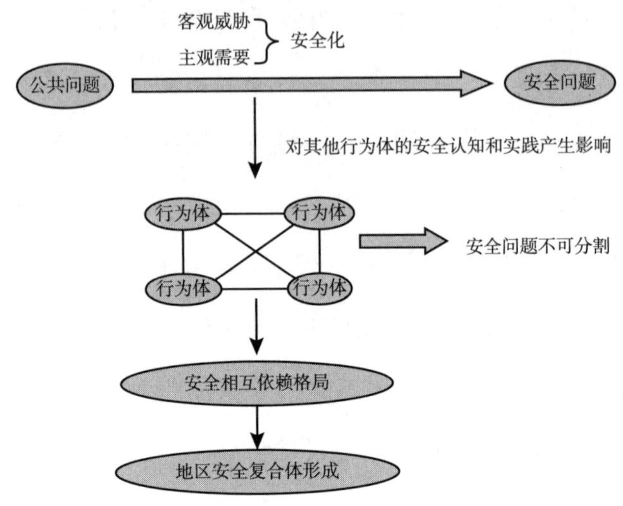

图 1　“安全化”与地区安全复合体形成

综上所述，根据大湄公河次区域的安全化及其进程，我们可以将湄公河次区域环境安全复合体定义为：“大湄公河次区域的各个国家，它们之间关于环境问题的安全化、去安全化过程或者二者紧密地联系在一起，以至于它们之间的环境问题不能被分割开解决。”

二　大湄公河次区域环境安全复合体的权力关系及其特征

依据地区安全复合体理论，权力关系决定了地区安全复合体的内核结构和特性。因此，对大湄公河次区域环境安全复合体的权力关系进行分析，有助于理解该复合体的内核结构特征。

权力是国际政治中现实主义流派的核心概念之一。权力应包括两方面内涵：一是客观的物质性实力，以经济实力和军事实力为核心；二是政治影响力，即一个国家能够影响或控制他人的意愿和能力。依据地区安全复合体理论，极性（权力关系）和社会性建构（友好/敌对模式）决定了安全复合体的内核结构和特性。极性原本是考察全球层次权力分配格局的变量，在地区安全复合体理论看来，极性同样适用于地区权力关系的分析。极性决定了安全复合体的权力关系，即复合体内部各单位的权力分配状况。从权力关系来看，大湄公河次区域形成了以次区域内部国家权力关系为核心、域外国家或区域形成外来干预变量的权力关系。其权力关系包含了多个安全组群的互动，其中主要有四个安全组群：次区域内部国家之间的权力关系、东盟对次区域权力关系的影响、日本对次区域权力关系的影响、全球超级大国美国对次区域权力关系的影响。此外，还有邻近区域一些地区大国比如印度、澳大利亚等国也对大湄公河次区域的权力关系形成干预变量。

1. 次区域国家间的权力关系

在大湄公河次区域环境安全复合体中，对复合体安全态势影响最大的是次区域国家间的权力关系，即包括中国在内的次区域其他国家间的权力关系。不管是从现有的经济实力、军事实力来看大湄公河次区域内各国家的权力分配状况，中国都在其中占据着一定的优势，次区域内其他国家除了泰国的经济实力稍强一些之外，其他国家都相对较弱。如果仅从硬实力来看，大湄公河次区域环境安全复合体形成了以中国为一极的单极的权力关系，应当属于中心化安全复合体中的大国地区安全复合体，即由一个全球层次的大国主导的地区安全复合体。但是，与美国主导的北美安全复合体和俄罗斯主导的独联体安全复合体明显不同的是，中国虽然在大湄公河次区域环境安全复合体中实力占据较大优势，却没有像美国和俄罗斯一样在其安全复合体内有绝对的控制力，能够绝对主导地区安全形势。由于中国在全球环境治理中的话语权和在大湄公河次区域环境问题的话语权都相当的薄弱，而且它也没有以自身实力优势去控制其他国家、获取区域内霸权的意图，因此，次区域国家间的关系决定了大湄公河次区域环境安全复合体并不是一个典型的中心化地区安全复合体。

2. 外来变量干预的权力关系

除了以中国为中心的权力关系之外，东盟、日本、美国、澳大利亚等域外力量也对大湄公河次区域的权力关系造成了影响。

美国是对湄公河流域影响最早的国家之一。作为这一区域合作机制最早的倡导者和捐资方，美国在此区域的影响一直都存在。只是随着美国的战略中心重新回到亚太地区，其对湄公河流域的关注比之前更多。在美国“亚太再平衡战略”中，东南亚是重要的战略重心，而湄公河流域的相关国家更被美国视为在东南亚的战略支点。美国著名智库战略与国际问题研究中心（CSIS）认为：“一个强大、一体化的东盟是维持美国在东南亚影响力的战略重点，而这需要一个独立、稳定、繁荣的下湄公河地区……近年来中国在湄公河采取了一系列开发援助行为，如果任其发展可能会导致其更富有进攻性的策略，增强其在次区域的影响力，宣传其价值观和规则。”① 同时，“美国 - 日本 - 东盟”三角战略关系、“美国 - 日本 - 越南”三角战略关系等说法随着美国“重返亚太”战略的实施不断涌现出来。因此，美国认为必须要加强对湄公河流域国家的相关援助，帮助其成长起来以维持美国在该区域的影响力和领导力，遏制中国进一步“扩张”的意图。目前美国在大湄公河次区域施加影响力的主要方式是通过发展政治经济关系、双边援助来促进美国与各个国家的双边关系；与此同时，努力加强美国在区域机制建设方面的领导作用。特朗普上台后，美国暂时还没有清晰的湄公河区域的战略。但特朗普多次在各个场合提出印太地区的战略构想，这很可能代表了在其任期内美国战略重点的方向。湄公河流域作为太平洋和印度洋交界的地方必将受到美国

① CSIS, “Washington Needs a New Approach to the Lower Mekong—the Next South China Sea”, https://www.csis.org/analysis/washington - needs - new - approach - lower - mekong— “ - next - south - china - sea”, 2018. 4. 19.

更多的战略关注。

对于东盟来说，大湄公河次区域五个国家都是东盟成员国。东盟的最终目标是实现各个国家经济社会的繁荣发展以及实现区域一体化。一个和平、繁荣的大湄公河次区域有利于东盟的长远发展，因此东盟对于促进大湄公河次区域的发展采取积极的政策，其中就包括环境领域的合作。在 1996 年，东盟与湄公河流域国家建立了东盟－湄公河流域开发合作（AMBDC）的平台，主要任务是促进湄公河流域的经济发展和社会各方面的进步。目前，东盟与中国在环境领域已建立起"中国－东盟环境保护合作中心"，环境领域的合作是中国与东盟合作的优先领域之一。[①] 中国所倡导建立的"澜沧江－湄公河环境合作中心"就在"中国－东盟环境保护合作中心"的平台下运作。总的来说，东盟对于大湄公河次区域环境安全的影响是积极的，有利于推动次区域环境"去安全化"、推动次区域环境安全机制的发展。

日本在二战结束后就借战败赔偿的理由重新介入湄公河流域，是对湄公河水资源开发和环境保护影响最大的区域外国家之一。日本对大湄公河次区域环境保护的援助包括日本政府的官方援助和日本企业界的经济投入。随着中国在这一区域影响

① 中国－东盟环境保护合作中心：《中国－东盟环境合作行动计划（2011～2013）》，http：//www. chinaaseanenv. org/dmhbhz/hzwj/201612/t20161226_ 373444. shtml，2018 年 4 月 23 日登录。

力的逐渐增大，以及美国的战略重心再次转到这一区域，日本将更加重视对湄公河流域的援助与合作，其影响将长期存在。日本对次区域环境安全的介入主要有几方面的考虑。第一，拓展自身的外交空间，加强日本在湄公河流域这一重要战略位置的存在。东南亚是战后日本重点发展的外交空间，通过对湄公河流域国家各方面的援助有利于保持并增强日本对东南亚地区的影响力。第二，实现平衡中国在这一地区影响力的战略目标。日本与中国在湄公河次区域的竞争主要在于各个领域机制建设的主导权。在环境领域，日本的国际话语权和相关的技术经验相对于中国优势都较为明显，因此日本在大湄公河次区域的环境安全机制建设和对相关国家的援助中影响力都非常大。第三，配合美国在这一区域的战略。日本在美国的一些对该地区的环境方面的援助中都充当着合作者甚至是“先锋”的角色。比如在美国提出的“湄公河下游倡议”中，日本就是一个积极的参与伙伴。总的来说，日本对于大湄公河次区域环境安全的介入主要有资金方面的援助、环保技术的输出、推动环境合作机制建设等，对于次区域环境保护做出了实际的行动，也有利于次区域环境安全机制的发展。

澳大利亚也是对大湄公河次区域环境安全参与度比较高的国家。冷战结束后，澳大利亚就意识到“融入亚洲”以在地缘政治和经济格局的剧烈变动之中获得国家利益的重要性，并把发展与东盟的关系作为融入亚洲的战略基石。湄公河流域在东盟和亚洲都拥有重要的战略地位，澳大利亚对湄公河流域的基本政策是通过多边合作机制促进该区域的地区整合和一体化。[①] 2007 年 9 月，澳大利亚出台《大湄公河次区域：澳大利亚促进其一体化和合作战略（2007～2011）》，报告指出通过非传统安全的多边合作，促进湄公河地区的整合和一体化符合澳大利亚在这一地区的国家利益。[②] 其中，促进湄公河流域的水资源治理和管理是澳大利亚援助该区域的重要领域。在 2007 年 9 月，澳大利亚还出台了《湄公河水资源战略报告（2007～2011）》。澳大利亚对湄公河流域的环境援助的主要措施有：成立与湄公河有关的研究机构，推动环境安全多边机制建设，提供湄公河水资源的相关数据和科学技术支持，与湄公河委员会进行合作（提供资金与科研的援助）等。[③] 最重要的是，澳大利亚试图在次区域建立一个能解决各国水资源争端的框架，以解决长久以来困扰各国的水资源利用问题。总的来说，澳大利亚对大湄公河次区域的区域一体化战略目标以及其具体的一些环境援助政策整体上有利于次区域多边环境安全机制的发展。

---

① 毕世鸿、王韶宇：《澳大利亚与湄公河五国关系的发展及其影响》，《大湄公河次区域合作发展报告 2014》，社会科学文献出版社，第 120 页。

② 毕世鸿、王韶宇：《澳大利亚与湄公河五国关系的发展及其影响》，《大湄公河次区域合作发展报告 2014》，社会科学文献出版社，第 120 页。

③ 毕世鸿、王韶宇：《澳大利亚与湄公河五国关系的发展及其影响》，《大湄公河次区域合作发展报告 2014》，社会科学文献出版社，第 122 页。

因此，大湄公河次区域环境安全复合体呈现以中国与其余五国关系为核心、多个外来变量干预这样由多个安全组群组成的权力结构。这样的权力关系对大湄公河次区域安全态势的影响是：中国的国内状况影响了地区层次的安全态势，而中国全球大国的身份又使得地区层次和其他地区以及全球层次有了更多的互动。

三 大湄公河次区域环境安全复合体的内核结构与社会性建构

当一个地区安全复合体，依据其单元之间的安全相互依存格局被界定出来之后，就可以对其内核结构和安全态势进行分析。依据地区安全复合体理论，地区安全复合体的内核结构有四个变量：边界、无政府结构、极性和社会性建构。边界主要是指地区安全复合体所包括的地理范围。无政府结构意味着地区安全复合体必须包括两个或以上的单元。极性是指安全复合体内各个单元权力分配的状况。社会性建构则是指这一地区各个单元之间的友好/敌对模式。其中极性（权力关系）和社会性建构决定了安全复合体的内核结构和特性。极性决定了安全复合体的权力关系，即复合体内部各单位的权力分配状况。社会性建构即各国之间的友好/敌对模式，通常是由地区内部产生的，受历史、政治和物质因素的影响。在巴里·布赞看来，友好/敌对模式有冲突形态、安全机制和安全共同体三种模式。

1. 边界

大湄公河次区域环境安全复合体包括了湄公河流域的五个国家和一个国家的两个地区，即缅甸、老挝、泰国、柬埔寨、越南，中国的云南省和广西壮族自治区，总面积为256.86万平方公里。北部是中国的广西壮族自治区和云南省；西北部是缅甸，通过印度与南亚次大陆接壤；西南边是泰国，毗邻安达曼海；东边是越南，毗邻南海相接太平洋西岸；南部是泰国与柬埔寨，连接中国南海。次区域总体位置处于亚洲东南部，西接南亚次大陆、东临南海、北靠中国、南临南海。其中大部分属于中南半岛。虽然湄公河只流经这些国家的其中一部分领土，但是缅甸、老挝、泰国、柬埔寨、越南领土的全部以及中国的云南省和广西壮族自治区都纳入整个大湄公河次区域的范围。

2. 无政府结构

从无政府结构来看，大湄公河次区域六个国家都是主权国家。这一区域没有超于主权国家之上的超国家机构来对各个国家进行管控。相反，这一区域大部分都是后殖民国家，国家主权对于它们来说是得之不易的，因此它们对于守卫国家主权的意愿是相当强烈的。这种主权国家政府间的互动组成了区域的一种无政府结构。

3. 极性

大湄公河次区域形成了以次区域内部国家权力关系为核心、域外国家或区域形成外来干预变量的权力关系，其权力关系包含了多个安全组群的互动，其中主要有四个安全组群：次区域内部国家之间的权力关系、东盟对次区域权力关系的影响、日本对次区域权力关系的影响、全球超级大国美国对次区域权力关系的影响。此外，还有临近区域一些地区大国比如印度、澳大利亚等国也对大湄公河次区域的权力关系形成干预变量。大湄公河次区域环境安全复合体目前呈现一种以中国为中心、多个外来变量干预的关系。这种多组群互动的权力关系对复合体安全态势的发展起到决定性作用。

4. 社会性建构

大湄公河次区域环境安全复合体，目前的社会性建构是安全机制模式。在相对温和的国家间关系、相对良好的自然资源和环境条件以及现有的环境安全机制的调节下，大湄公河次区域环境安全复合体得以避免像约旦河流域、尼罗河流域等区域因水资源和环境所引发的严重冲突。大湄公河次区域各方力量在环境问题上还存在许多分歧，尤其是上下游对于水坝建设的不同声音，但总体来看该区域因环境问题而发生严重斗争的可能性微乎其微，环境安全机制在地区合作的总体框架下朝着更深层次的合作发展。

根据布赞的地区安全复合体理论，一个地区安全复合体的内核结构除了权力关系，还由社会性建构来界定。社会性建构即友好/敌对模式，地区安全复合体是由持久的友好/敌对模式界定的。依据哥本哈根学派的理论，地区安全复合体的社会性建构有三种模式：冲突形态、安全机制和安全共同体。冲突形态是指成员之间把彼此作为威胁，一旦有必要可以使用武力解决问题。安全机制是指成员之间仍把彼此视为潜在的威胁，但已建立起一定的规则制度来约束彼此的行为，使用武力的期望降低，安全困境被弱化。安全共同体是指成员之间已经建立起完全的信任，坚信它们之间不会使用武力去解决问题。

依据三种模式的内涵来看，大湄公河次区域环境安全的一个重要特征就是，虽然行为体因为某些原因把环境问题安全化了，但这种安全相互依存格局没有造成严重的冲突。相反，大湄公河次区域环境安全复合体从它萌发直至形成发展至今的过程来看一直都有较为稳固的机制在维系彼此的合作，虽然其中夹杂着弱的冲突，但总的来看次区域的社会性建构最起码不是敌对的。美国俄勒冈州立大学水资源数据库的统计数据表明，与两河流域、约旦河流域、尼罗河流域明显不同的是，湄公河流域的冲突形态一直都是很弱的，而且冲突焦点主要集中在航运、水电等领域。[①] 大湄公河次区域环境安全复合体能保持一

① 王志坚：《水霸权、安全秩序与制度构建——国际河流水政治复合体研究》，社会科学文献出版社，2015，第64～67页。

种较为温和的友好合作模式，并呈现出较为成熟的环境安全复合体的合作机制，主要有以下几个原因。

第一，湄公河流域水资源稀缺程度和生态环境恶化不至于很严重，各个成员国还未出现为了生存而进行严重的斗争情况。与两河流域、约旦河流域和尼罗河流域等极度干旱缺水的地区相比，湄公河流域的水资源状况还算比较稳定。湄公河流域的生态环境比如森林覆盖率、气候、水文水系状况、耕地质量都比一些环境恶劣的国际河流流域要好，水资源紧缺和环境恶化所引起的生存威胁没有约旦河流域、两河流域等地区迫切。因此，湄公河流域没有发生过为了争夺水资源或生态环境矛盾而爆发的严重冲突。

第二，相比两河流域、约旦河流域、尼罗河流域和恒河流域的国家间关系，湄公河流域各国之间的关系相对比较友好，没有把彼此视为敌人。虽然次区域各国的意识形态、社会制度、文化价值观各不相同，但是冷战结束以来它们之间并没有爆发过严重的国家间冲突。导致这些国家间相对平和的关系的原因有以下几点。首先，次区域各国间没有很深的历史积怨和宗教矛盾。历史上各国之间没有严重的国家仇恨记忆和集体仇恨记忆。虽然说近代以来尤其是冷战期间一些国家之间发生了不愉快甚至是战争，但目前来看它们都没有把对方当作不能共存的敌人。次区域也没有像中东那样错综复杂的宗教关系。其次，东盟的作用非常重要。东盟当时的建立就是为了解决各成员国内部的问题以及协调彼此之间的关系来维护地区的稳定与发展。在东盟框架的指引下，东盟国家之间逐渐朝着“安全化”趋势发展，彼此都愿意为了地区的稳定发展和平共处。阿查亚认为到20世纪90年代初，东盟已经超越了权力政治，成员国没有陷入安全困境和军备竞赛中，不再使用武力彼此对抗，而是寻求通过和平方式解决争议与冲突。[①] 因此，次区域各国虽然仍有矛盾存在，但它们已不再把彼此视为敌人。最后，该区域不存在霸权国，也不存在霸权体系的权力关系。约旦河流域的以色列、尼罗河流域的埃及、两河流域的土耳其、恒河流域的印度都不同程度上在其流域内推行一定的霸权行为，而这些流域的国家间关系的复杂性使得它们很容易用激烈的手段去反击霸权国的行为，从而经常造成严重的冲突。中国虽然从硬实力来看的确是大湄公河次区域国家中最强大的，但目前来看中国并没有在次区域推行霸权行为，并没有企图就地理位置优势、综合实力优势来对其他国家进行政治上的控制。因此，次区域内国家间在环境安全问题上得以以一种较为和平的方式解决问题。

第三，湄公河流域很早之前就逐渐形成了一些合作机制，比如湄公河委员会。这些合作机制能够在安全态势演进的过程中促进成员国彼此间的信任，也能够作为一些潜在的冲突事件

① 转引自季玲《历史、实践与东盟安全合作进程》，《外交评论》2014年第5期，第87~88页。

缓冲器。目前该区域主要的环境合作机制有大湄公河次区域经济合作机制平台下的环境合作机制、湄公河委员会和澜沧江－湄公河合作机制下的环境合作平台。湄公河委员会是这些环境合作机制中历史最悠久的一个，也是唯一主要以水资源以及环境的综合开发和可持续发展为宗旨的机制。除了湄公河委员会之外，第一个包含湄公河流域所有国家的合作机制的大湄公河次区域经济合作机制由亚洲开发银行于1992年倡导建立，成员国包括了次区域内所有六个国家。在1995年，GMS正式把环境确立为合作平台下的一个重要合作领域。中国在2015年倡导建立了包含六个国家在内的澜沧江—湄公河合作机制，并于2016年3月在澜沧江—湄公河合作首次领导人会议上提出设立澜沧江—湄公河环境合作中心的构想。这些环境合作机制各存在一些不足，但它们为次区域各方力量解决环境安全问题提供了协商合作的平台，同时一定程度上对各方的行动提供了制度和规则的约束力。

总之，大湄公河次区域由于环境问题的“安全化”与“去安全化”，其进程紧密相连，不可分割开来加以解决，因而导致了大湄公河次区域安全复合体的形成。其内核结构呈现出以中国为中心的，域外国家干预介入的复合型大国中心结构，其社会性建构模式，已经属于较为成熟的环境安全合作机制的模式。随着东盟共同体的构建，大湄公河次区域环境安全复合体也将呈现出向环境安全共同体发展的趋向。

经济走廊与澜湄发展走廊

“一带一路”与泰国东部走廊发展计划对接的机遇、挑战与建议

宋清润　常　翔*

摘　要：“中泰一家亲”，双方关系长期友好，已经建立全面战略合作伙伴关系，经贸等领域的合作密切。目前，中国“一带一路”倡议与泰国东部经济走廊发展规划正在加强对接合作，存在诸多机遇，当然，也存在不少挑战，有些挑战较难克服。笔者提出一些推动双方重大合作的建议，如，两国都应该优化向对方宣传己方发展规划的方式，两国在合作中都更应该注重“舒适度”原则，两国都要更重视推动民间交流，两国要重视联合培养更多符合两国合作需要的合格人才。

* 宋清润，中国现代国际关系研究院美国所副研究员、博士；常翔，广西玉林师范学院泰国研究中心特聘研究员、中心副主任。

关键词： 中国　“一带一路”倡议　泰国　东部经济走廊

泰国是东南亚重要国家，中国是亚洲以及世界上的重要国家。中泰两国有着长期友好合作关系，我们经常说“中泰一家亲”。近年来，中泰两国合作推进“一带一路”建设，取得一定成果。近来，泰国高度重视实施东部经济走廊发展规划，并将其作为与“一带一路”倡议对接合作的重点板块。2018年8月24日，泰国总理巴育会见赴泰主持中泰经贸联委会第六次会议的中国国务委员王勇。王勇表示，中方愿同泰方一道，落实好两国领导人重要共识，加强“一带一路”倡议同泰国“东部经济走廊”等发展战略对接。巴育表示，泰方高度重视泰中友好，支持并愿积极参与“一带一路”建设，泰方愿同中方加强投资、教育、科技、基础设施、电子商务等领域合作，欢迎中国企业参与“东部经济走廊”建设，拓展两国务实合作范围。[①] 目前及将来，中国“一带一路”倡议与泰国东部经济走廊发展规划作为两国合作提供新的机遇。本文将分析中国“一带一路”倡议与泰国东部经济走廊发展规划对接合作的机遇、挑战，并提出相关建议。

① 《泰国总理巴育会见王勇》，中国政府网，2018年8月24日，http：//www. gov. cn/guowuyuan/2018－08/24/content_ 5316430. htm。

一 机遇

中国“一带一路”实施5年来，已经取得较大成就。2013年9月和10月由中国国家主席习近平分别提出建设“新丝绸之路经济带”和“21世纪海上丝绸之路”的合作倡议，也就是“一带一路”合作倡议。2015年3月28日，经中国国务院授权，中国国家发展改革委、外交部、商务部联合发布了《推动共建丝绸之路经济带和21世纪海上丝绸之路的愿景与行动》。这份官方发布的“一带一路”文件指出：“‘一带一路’”建设是一项系统工程，要坚持共商、共建、共享原则，积极推进沿线国家发展战略的相互对接。‘一带一路’是促进共同发展、实现共同繁荣的合作共赢之路，是增进理解信任、加强全方位交流的和平友谊之路。中国政府倡议，秉持和平合作、开放包容、互学互鉴、互利共赢的理念，全方位推进务实合作，打造政治互信、经济融合、文化包容的利益共同体、命运共同体和责任共同体。‘一带一路’贯穿亚欧非大陆，一头是活跃的东亚经济圈，一头是发达的欧洲经济圈，中间广大腹地国家经济发展潜力巨大。丝绸之路经济带重点畅通中国经中亚、俄罗斯至欧洲（波罗的海）；中国经中亚、西亚至波斯湾、地中海；中国至东南亚、南亚、印度洋。21世纪海上丝绸之路重点方向是从中国沿海港口过南海到印度洋，延伸至欧洲；从中国沿海港口过南海到南太平洋。‘一带一路’合作以政策沟通、设施联通、贸易畅通、资金融通、民心相通为主要内容。”① 2017 年国际合作高峰论坛一共形成了 279 项成果清单，目前已经有 255 项转为常态化工作，有 24 项工作正在有序推进。截至 2018 年 5 月中旬，中国已与 88 个国家和国际组织签署了 103 份共建“一带一路”倡议合作文件。②

泰国“东部经济走廊”发展规划刚刚起步。泰国 2017 年上半年通过东部经济走廊发展规划，下半年正式推动走廊建设。走廊建设主要是推动泰国产业升级转型，提升国家竞争力，推动解决国家经济社会发展中的多种问题。走廊包括曼谷周边的北柳府、春武里府、罗勇府等三府，地处泰国湾东岸，位于泰国传统的东部工业发达地区，规划总面积 13266 平方公里，其中，工业用地总规划面积超过 48 平方公里。走廊建设周期是2017～2021 年，要发展新一代汽车制造、智能电子等高新产业，还要扩建或新建一批码头、铁路、公路、机场等一批基础设施。③ 走廊建设的各类项目总预算约 430 亿美元，其

① 《授权发布：推动共建丝绸之路经济带和 21 世纪海上丝绸之路的愿景与行动》，新华网，2015 年 3 月 28 日，http：//www. xinhuanet. com/world/2015－03/28/c_ 1114793986. htm。

② 《“一带一路”国际合作高峰论坛成果已完成 255 项》，搜狐网，2018 年 5 月 17 日，http：//www. sohu. com/a/231982493_ 165665。

③ 常翔、张锡镇：《泰国东部经济走廊发展规划》，《东南亚纵横》2017 年第 4 期，第 14～17 页。

中，政府计划投资占投资总规划的约1/5，其余资金则需要引入民间资本和外资。2017 年开始，乌塔堡机场扩建、林查班港口扩建等先期项目已经开始建设。①

下文分析一下中国"一带一路"倡议与泰国"东部经济走廊"发展规划在对接合作方面的主要机遇。

总体而言，在过去四五年时间里，中国与泰国在"一带一路"建设合作方面，表现较好。限于篇幅，此处不一一列举具体成果，主要采用北京大学"一带一路"五通指数研究课题组发布的《"一带一路"沿线国家五通指数报告》(2017) 中的数据。该数据指出，在研究涉及的 60 多个沿线国家的五通指数中，泰国总排名为第六，在东盟十国中则排名第三。这个数据充分说明了中泰两国在"一带一路"合作上的密切程度。②

两国官方目前都高度重视中国"一带一路"倡议与泰国东部经济走廊发展规划的对接与合作。"一带一路"倡议自 2013 年提出以来，在目前及将来，长期是中国与沿线国家合

---

① "'Eastern Economic Corridor Development project' Driving Forward…", Ministry of Industry, Thailand, February 15, 2017, http://www.boi.go.th/upload/EEC%20pack%20for%20BOI%20fair_Rev4%203%201.pdf.

② 《2017 中国－东盟"五通指数"出炉　新马泰位居前三》，中国新闻网，2017 年 12 月 8 日，http://www.chinanews.com/gj/2017/12-08/8395892.shtml。"一带一路"五通主要指：政策沟通、设施联通、贸易畅通、资金融通、民心相通。

作的“关键倡议”，有助于中国与沿线国家提升合作，共建命运共同体。因此，中国投入大量精力和资源与沿线国家共建“一带一路”。泰国方面，目前投入大量精力和资源，积极向国内外宣传走廊建设，谋求与他国合作，共同推动泰国东部经济走廊建设。如何调动国内外资源来助推东部经济走廊建设，是泰国目前对外经济合作的重点。因此，中国与泰国的对外合作倡议（规划）有了很多契合之处，将两大倡议（规划）的对接作为双方合作的重中之重，因为，泰国是东盟重要国家，是中国在东盟的重要合作伙伴，两国已经建立全面战略合作伙伴关系，而中国是泰国的第一大贸易伙伴国和重要外资来源国，是泰国重要的基础设施建设合作国。

当两国官方重视推进中国“一带一路”倡议与泰国东部经济走廊发展规划的对接与合作时，自然预示着两国经贸合作的前景会更好，各种合作机会更多，自然也会激励两国商界和企业更积极参与两国经贸合作。企业是两国经贸合作的主体。这样就会形成两国官方和企业合作良性互动、相得益彰的局面。

泰国经济走廊发展规划涉及的一些重要产业与中国制造2025的一些重要产业有不少相似之处，而且，泰国东部经济走廊高度重视基础设施建设和走廊建设涉及区域内的互联互通，这与“一带一路”建设也有很多契合点与合作点。

泰国经济走廊发展规划重点发展一些产业，以提升泰国经济竞争力，实现泰国经济4.0发展目标。该发展规划涉及的一些重要产业有：先进的生物与农业科技产业、食品加工业、高端健康与医疗产业、旅游业、先进的石油化工和生化项目、航空产业、物流产业、电动汽车和无人驾驶汽车产业、智能电子产业、机器人产业，等等。①中国制造2025年重点发展的一些产业有：新一代信息技术产业、新一代信息技术产业、航空航天装备、海洋工程装备及高技术船舶、先进轨道交通装备、节能与新能源汽车、电力装备、农机装备、新材料、生物医药及高性能医疗器械，等等。② 同时，泰国经济走廊重视发展一批大型基础设施建设项目，比如，乌塔堡机场扩建，曼谷-罗勇高铁和东部地区复线铁路升级项目、林查班港口扩建、马达普港口扩建、城市水电道路基础设施、城际公路，等等。③ 而中国与沿线国家共建"一带一路"的重要领域也是基础设施与互联互通项目。由此可见，双方的重大产业发展规划和对外合作的一些重点领域，有较多契合点，带来了新的合作机遇。尤

① "Eastern Economic Corridor (EEC)", Royal Thai Embassy, Washington D. C. , http://thaiembdc.org/eastern-economic-corridor-eec/, last accessed on August 6, 2018.

② 《国务院关于印发〈中国制造2025〉的通知》，工业和信息化部，2015年5月19日，http://www.miit.gov.cn/n973401/n1234620/n1234622/c4409653/content.html。

③ "Eastern Economic Corridor (EEC)", Royal Thai Embassy, Washington D. C. , http://thaiembdc.org/eastern-economic-corridor-eec/, last accessed on August 6, 2018.

其是，泰国东部经济走廊重视发展一批大型基础设施项目，其自身在资金、技术、人才等方面存在困难，比如，2017～2021年，泰国东部经济走廊计划建设的重大基础设施项目有多个，规划投资如下：乌塔堡机场扩建计划投资57亿美元，马达普港口扩建计划投资3亿美元，林查班港口扩建25亿美元，高铁计划投资45亿美元，新城市建设与医院建设115亿美元，旅游业设施等建设计划投资57亿美元，公路建设10亿美元，复线铁路建设18亿美元，共计330亿美元。[①] 这是个宏大的发展与投资规划，不仅需要大量的资金，也需要大量的企业、设备、人员等参与，单纯靠泰国一己之力是较难实现的，需要争取国外的资金、技术、人才等方面的支持。而中国企业在基础设施建设方面有着丰富的资金、技术、装备与人才等，有着丰富的国际合作经验，而且，也希望拓展国际市场，希望提升国际竞争力。因此，中泰政府和企业在建设泰国东部经济走廊方面有着广阔的合作空间。

中泰目前经济发展态势均较好，这为中国“一带一路”倡议与泰国“东部经济走廊”发展规划的对接合作提供了非常好的大环境，加之，美国贸易保护主义盛行，与中国以及印

① “‘Eastern Economic Corridor Development project’ Driving Forward...”, Ministry of Industry, Thailand, February 15, 2017, http://www.boi.go.th/upload/EEC% 20pack% 20for% 20BOI% 20fair_ Rev4% 203% 201.pdf.

尼等部分东盟国家产生贸易摩擦，也促使中国与泰国等东盟国家更加重视推动亚洲区域内的经贸合作，来缓解美国贸易保护主义的不利影响。

泰国是东盟国家中仅次于印尼的第二大经济体，2017 年 GDP 增速为 3.9%，比 2016 年 3.3% 的增速要快些，是 2012 年以来增速最高的一年。① 2018 年第一季度 GDP 增长 4.8%，政府预计当年全年 GDP 增速为 4.2%。这就意味着泰国有所摆脱前几年经济增速不高的局面。② 泰国经济表现有所变好，意味着其对外经济合作的活跃度也会增强。同时，泰国近年来的投资环境也变得更好。世界银行发布了《2018 年全球营商环境报告》指出，泰国成为东盟国家中最吸引外资的国家之一，在吸引外资环境的排名中，位居东盟十国的前三名，在全球的排名则从 2016 年的第 46 名上升至第 26 名。③ 而且，泰国在东南亚的地理位置优越，是连接东盟陆地国家（也是常说的中南半岛的缅甸、越南、老挝、柬埔寨等国）与东盟海岛国家

① Yukako Ono, "Thailand's GDP grows at fastest pace in 5 years in 2017", Nikkei, February 19, 2018, https://asia.nikkei.com/Economy/Thailand-s-GDP-grows-at-fastest-pace-in-5-years-in-2017.

② "Thailand GDP Annual Growth Rate 1994 - 2018", Trading Economics, https://tradingeconomics.com/thailand/gdp-growth-annual (Acccessed on June 25, 2018).

③ Vasundhara Rastog, "Thailand's Investment Outlook for 2018", ASEAN Briefing, February 27, 2018, https://www.aseanbriefing.com/news/2018/02/27/thailands-investment-outlook-2018.html.

（也称海洋国家，指菲律宾、马来西亚、文莱、印尼、新加坡等国）的枢纽，连接着区域的多个国家的生产基地和市场。

如上文所述，泰国东部经济走廊建设预计总投资超过400多亿美元，泰国政府自身难以投资如此多的资金去建设走廊，因为其自身经济规模不是很大，政府债务较高。根据国际货币基金组织的数据，2017年，泰国GDP为4550亿美元，政府当年总投资额占GDP的23%，约为1050亿美元，而当年政府总债务占GDP约42%，约为1910亿美元。[①] 因此，泰国建设东部经济走廊必须借助招商引资的渠道，要借助外资支持。2018年2月，泰国出台新的法律，推出更多优惠政策来吸引外资帮助泰国建设东部经济走廊。这些优惠包括，泰国会对参与东部经济走廊建设的投资者减税，允许投资者在走廊建设地区可以租地99年，并将简化投资企业相关人员赴泰的签证手续，加快投资审批速度，增强服务质量。[②] 这些优惠措施也会吸引更多中国企业投资。

---

① Please see http://www.imf.org/external/pubs/ft/weo/2018/01/weodata/weorept.aspx? sy=2017&ey=2018&scsm=1&ssd=1&sort=country&ds=.&br=1&pr1.x=68&pr1.y=16&c=578&s=NGDPD%2CNID_NGDP%2CGGXWDG_NGDP%2CBCA%2CBCA_NGDPD&grp=0&a=, last accessed on June 26, 2018.

② "Thailand approves law for $45 billion Eastern Economic Corridor", Reuters, February 8, 2018, https://www.reuters.com/article/us-thailand-investment/thailand-approves-law-for-45-billion-eastern-economic-corridor-idUSKBN1FS24B.

中国是亚洲最大经济体和世界第二大经济体，近年来，中国年均经济增速总体保持较高水平，比如，2017 年，中国 GDP 增速为 6.9%。[①] 中国有着巨大的市场，近年来正在与沿线国家共建“一带一路”，对外投资也总体居于高位，比如，中国非金融领域的对外投资总额为 1830 亿美元，成为世界第二大外资输出国。2017 年，中国对外投资总额为 1200 亿美元，降幅较大的原因主要是中资在美欧等西方国家遭遇更多的投资壁垒。[②] 因此，中国企业对外投资近一两年来更重视投向东盟国家等发展中国家，而泰国是东盟国家中较好的投资目的地，是中国在东盟国家中投资较多的国家。截至 2017 年 2 月，中国企业在泰国获得批准的投资项目共计 607 个，总投资额达 66.73 亿美元。[③] 在 2018 年，中国企业对泰国投资中较为重要是一个例子是，4 月，中国阿里巴巴网络技术有限公司（简称：阿里巴巴集团）宣布向泰国投资 3.2 亿美元，以推动中泰

① 《统计局：2017 年中国 GDP 总量超 82 万亿全年增速 6.9%》，新浪网，2018 年 1 月 18 日，http://finance.sina.com.cn/china/hgjj/2018-01-18/doc-ifyqquptv7644897.shtml。

② 《2017 年我国对外投资规模达 1200 亿美元》，新华网，2018 年 1 月 16 日，http://www.xinhuanet.com/fortune/2018-01/16/c_1122267906.htm。

③ 《〈泰国蓝皮书〉：中国对泰国直接投资发展迅速》，光明日报客户端，2017 年 11 月 10 日，http://world.gmw.cn/2017-11/10/content_26751759.htm。

电商产业合作，这为两国新兴产业合作提供了强劲动力。① 当前及未来，随着泰国东部经济走廊建设的推进，随着配套走廊建设出台的一系列招商引资优惠措施的逐步落实，中企赴泰国投资者会更多。

中国和日本是亚洲两大经济体，近期，两国关系有所改善，双方为避免在东南亚等国家出现两国企业的恶性竞争，尤其是在基础设施领域避免恶性竞争，2018 年 5 月 9 日，中日签署《关于中日第三方市场合作的备忘录》，决定设立跨部门的“推进中日第三方市场合作工作机制”。两国有关部门正在磋商在泰国合作修建曼谷轻轨铁路事宜，同时，连接曼谷素万那普机场至中部城市的高铁建设项目也在讨论之中。② 因此，目前及未来，中国、日本与泰国三方可以在泰国东部经济走廊的铁路、公路以及其他城市建设项目上开展合作，创造一个三赢的局面。

二　挑战

如上文所述，中国“一带一路”倡议与泰国“东部经济

① Patpicha Tanakasempipat, “Alibaba to invest $320 million in Thailand, as rivals boost presence”, Reuters, APRIL 19, 2018, https://www.reuters.com/article/us-alibaba-thailand/alibaba-to-invest-320-million-in-thailand-as-rivals-boost-presence-idUSKBN1HQ1B.

② 《中日将就“一带一路”合作日媒：首个项目是泰国轻轨》，参考消息网，2018 年 7 月 21 日，http://www.cankaoxiaoxi.com/world/20180721/2296416.shtml?bsh_bid=2239650751。

走廊”发展规划的对接合作存在诸多机遇，但毋庸讳言，也存在不少挑战，有些挑战是长期的，较难彻底解决。

泰国东部经济走廊建设是泰国有史以来投资规模最大的系统发展规划，涉及诸多大小项目，需要历经多年才能完成。其中走廊建设规划的工业用地就达 48 平方公里，铁路、公路等其他一些基础设施等项目也要占地。而泰国土地制度是以私有制为主体，政府拥有的土地不及民众拥有的土地。因此，东部经济走廊建设涉及大量征地势必引发拆迁、补偿等纠纷，可能引发民众的不满乃至抗议示威行为。泰国有专家和媒体指出，在新的关于东部经济走廊的法律框架下，政府部门有权绕过现行的一些法律规定而加快外资审批速度，政府部门在东部经济走廊涉及的征地、资源、环境等方面的管理不善，并且有时为了吸引外资项目而忽视环保问题，引发的问题较多。[①] 随着泰国东部经济走廊建设的推进，随着更多国内外投资者进入当地开展项目，当地地价正在升高。同时，泰国近年来的环境退化问题也较为严重，引发的社会关注度很高。比如，近年来，泰国森林面积年均减少 1600 平方公里，矿产资源也有过度开发。[②] 其实，泰国公民社会发达，非政府组织数量众多且十分

① “EEC law ‘harms local people’”, *The Nation*, May 16, 2018, http://www.nationmultimedia.com/detail/national/30345484.

② 常翔、张锡镇：《泰国东部经济走廊发展规划》，《东南亚纵横》2017 年第 4 期，第 15 页。

活跃，民众权利意识强烈，征地问题、环保问题是近年来泰国社会的热点议题。如何平衡经济发展与资源环境保护问题，是泰国的一大难题。如果东部经济走廊造成一批失地民众，而他们又对政府补偿方案不满或者没有获得妥善安置的话，那么，就会产生纠纷，产生抗议示威活动。因此，泰国能否解决好东部经济走廊目前以及未来会产生的征地问题，也会影响到当地社会稳定，影响到中泰企业在东部经济走廊建设方面的合作，尤其是会影响到一些重大基础设施项目的合作，因为这些项目基本都占地较多。

中泰在东部经济走廊建设建设中的合作项目会增多，用工量也会增多，产业工人缺乏，尤其是合格的技术工人缺乏问题恐是中泰诸多合作项目顺利推进和运营的挑战之一。

中国人口老龄化问题近年来日益突出。2017 年，中国有约 2.4 亿年龄超过 60 岁的老龄人口，占中国总人口的 17.3%，其中，仅在 2017 年，中国老龄人口就增长了 1000 万。到 2050 年，中国老龄人口预计会达 4.87 亿，占中国当时总人口的约 34.9%。[①] 由此可见，中国老龄化问题将日益严重，劳动力缺乏问题也在日益显现。很多工厂、机构找不到合格、足量的工人，工人工资上涨较快。

---

① 《应对老龄化，看首都北京如何“攻坚”》，新华网，2018 年 6 月 22 日，http://www.xinhuanet.com/politics/2018-06/22/c_1123019097.htm。

同时，近年来，泰国劳动力缺乏的问题也日益突出。泰国国家经济与社会发展委员会的数据显示：2005 年以来，泰国人口老龄化问题就更加严重了，因为其 60 岁及以上的老龄人口明显持续增长，2017 年，泰国老龄人口总量为 1123 万，占全国总人口的 17.13%；到 2012 年，泰国将全面进入老龄化社会，该年度，泰国老龄人口将达 1310 万，占全国总人口的 20%。[①] 因此，近年来，泰国劳动力短缺的状况也日益凸显，一些工厂无法共用到足量且技能好的工人。以前，泰国工资水平比缅甸、老挝、柬埔寨等邻国的工资水平高很多，几百万邻国工人涌入泰国工作，一度弥补了泰国劳工短缺的状况。但是，近年来，泰国邻国的经济发展较快，工厂增多，工资上涨，加之泰国部分老板虐待外国工人的丑闻频频爆出，导致缅甸、老挝、柬埔寨等国部分工人纷纷回国工作。上述这些因素叠加，加剧了泰国劳动短缺的状况。

因此，中泰在泰国东部经济走廊推进的合作项目和企业如何能找到足量且技能好的工人，也会遇到难题。中国企业要外派工人到国外工作，则需要提供比国内高很多的工资，大概是需要支付国内工资的 3 倍左右甚至更高的工资，负担很重。而且，泰国是否会允许较多中国工人赴泰国工作，也是个问题，

① Wichit Chaitrong, “Risks grow for ageing population”, *The Nation*, December 11, 2017, http://www.nationmultimedia.com/detail/Economy/30333636.

因为这会影响到部分泰国人的就业，会引发泰国人和舆论的不满。而泰国国内工人供给不足，原先在泰国工作的邻国劳工有更多人陆续回国工作。这些因素叠加，势必增加中泰在泰国东部经济走廊合作项目的用工难度。

此外，在高端科技人才方面，中国高新科技产业领域的人才总体比泰国多很多，而泰国国内教育体系长期重视文科，忽视理工科的投入，导致国内大学毕业生中，文科生居多，而科技人才不足，不仅较难满足泰国自身高新技术产业发展的需要，而且，泰国东部经济走廊要发展一批高新技术产业，会吸引中资与泰国企业开展高新产业领域的合作，泰国高新技术人才的缺口会更大，中泰高新技术人员的有效对接合作估计会存在困难，需要磨合，甚至需要中国高新企业专门去培训一批对口专业领域的泰国高新技术人员，以便推动双方企业更好合作。

中泰铁路合作在过去 6 年历经起起伏伏，截至 2018 年 8 月，实际建设的只是首段 3.5 公里。这对中泰在东部经济走廊大型基础设施建设恐有负面影响，尤其是中国企业对投资泰国大型基础设施建设或有担忧，因为泰国东部经济走廊也有诸多投资大、耗时长的大型基础设施项目。

2012 年 4 月，泰国总理英拉访华时，亲身体验北京往返天津之间的高铁，有了引进中国高铁的想法。同年 10 月，李克强总理访问泰国，两国签署《中泰政府关于泰国铁路基础设施发展与泰国农产品交换的政府间合作项目谅解备忘录》，也就是“大米换高铁”协议。然而，2014 年 5 月，英拉被迫下台，巴育将军领导的军人政府随后上台，其与中国合作建设铁路的意愿仍在，但双方更改双方的铁路合作方案，涉及线路、涉及速度、投融资模式、中方贷款利率、铁路沿线开发权等多方面的变化。2017 年底，中泰达成的铁路建设一期工程为曼谷至呵叻段，全长约 253 公里，设计最高时速 250 公里，预计 2021 年通车。一期工程分 4 段逐步开工，分别长 3.5 公里、11 公里、119.5 公里和 119 公里。2017 年 12 月 21 日，中泰铁路合作项目一期工程开工仪式举行，此次开工的正是首段长 3.5 公里的线路，后续路段开工仍待时间。二期工程则是从呵叻至廊开，全线长约 355 公里，估计可能需要更多年时间才能建设。[①] 由此可见，中泰铁路在过去六年多时间里历经波折，进展不畅。中泰铁路未来发展前景的好坏对中国企业投资泰国大型基建项目势必带来影响，或是积极影响，或是消极影响。未来，中泰在泰国东部经济走廊其他项目上的合作如何趋利避害，减少波折，是个不容忽视的挑战。

泰国巴育政府从 2014 年开始执政，已经 4 年了，其最初承诺 2015 年举行大选，但实际上，因为多种原因，截至 2018

① 明大军、杨舟：《中泰铁路合作项目一期工程正式开工》，新华网，2017 年 12 月 21 日，http://www.xinhuanet.com/2017-12/21/c_1122149108.htm。

年8月，大选仍未举行，不少人士和团体呼吁当局尽快举行大选。巴育曾说要在2019年2月举行大选，但各方估计，因为多种因素的影响，大选日期恐会推迟，没个准数。[①] 但不论如何，不管是2019年举行大选，还是2020年或者更迟举行大选，大选是越来越近了，因为在野多个党派对巴育政府施加越来越大的压力。各方势力势必要抓住多年来难得的机会来争取更多政治权益，已经在布局大选，甚至已经有了多种形式的准备活动，泰国政坛博弈势必日益进入复杂的时期。大选前后的泰国政府是否稳定，未来新的民选政府是否会100%执行现政府的东部经济走廊发展规划，是否会严格执行现政府与中国在东部经济走廊建设方面达成的一些既有合同，尚待观察。

中泰综合国力差距日益拉大，中国是个世界级大国，而泰国是个中小型国家。比如，在GDP方面，2017年，中国GDP约为12万亿美元，而泰国同期仅为4550亿美元（当然，泰国人口也比中国少很多），中国GDP是泰国的26倍多。而且，未来，中国GDP每年增量与泰国GDP每年增量的差距也会越拉越大。因此，笔者这几年与泰国人交流时，也明显感觉到，

① Aukkarapon Niyomyat, Pracha Hariraksapitak, "Thailand signals election could be delayed until May", Reuters, June 25, 2018, https://www.reuters.com/article/us-thailand-politics/thailand-signals-election-could-be-delayed-until-may-idUSKBN1JL15P.

尽管中国人一再解释中国无意欺压或控制泰国，但有些泰国人对中国壮大的担忧有所增加，比如，其认为中国推进“一带一路”的目的中，扩张中国地缘政治影响力是首要目的，而经济合作收益则是次要的。还有些泰国人担心吸引中国投资过多导致中国企业对泰国经济影响力过大，导致更多中国人在泰国工作，等等。[①] 因此，泰国人在东部经济走廊建设方面的对华合作心态，也有着“期望与疑虑”的复杂心情。

影响中泰合作关系的第三方因素方面，美国、印度、日本、澳大利亚等国正在积极推进“印太战略”从改变转化为行动，而泰国是上述四国争取的重点国家之一，这四国未来恐会想方设法挤压中国在泰国的影响力，干扰中泰合作。美国国务卿蓬佩奥 2018 年 8 月上旬参加东亚外长会期间，数日内提出两项加强与东南亚、南亚相关国家合作的支持资金方案：一项是美国承诺为印太地区投入 1.13 亿美元，重点支持该地区部分国家的数字经济、能源和基础设施的发展；另一项是美国国务卿蓬佩奥宣布美国再“追加”3 亿美元安保资金投入，主要用于强化印太区域海事安全、人道主义救援、提升维护和平和应对跨国威胁能力。这加剧外界对美国将“印太战略”具

① 笔者 2018 年 8 月 9～14 日赴泰国参加第七届中泰战略研讨会期间，在听取泰国学者发言时，以及与泰国学者讨论中泰关系时，再次明显感受到泰国人对华的“既合作，又提防”的纠结心态。

体化，从而抗衡中国“一带一路”倡议的猜测。[①] 而泰国是美国盟国，尽管其并不像澳大利亚等美国盟国那样积极支持“印太战略”，但也势必是美国重点拉拢的对象，以便美国等国加快实施“印太战略”。在美国拉拢泰国的过程中，美国势必也会伺机干扰中泰间的一些合作项目，以削弱中国在泰国的影响力，增加美国在泰国的影响力。

三 工作建议

中泰均应该优化各自向彼此宣传对外合作倡议或规划的方式。目前，两国基本是各自向对方宣传自己的对外合作倡议或规划，是个单独行为，即中国人一般是单独向泰国介绍“一带一路”合作倡议，泰国人则是单独向中国人介绍东部经济走廊发展规划，两国官员和专家很难做到经常性地一起现场向两国媒体、商界等介绍两国对外合作倡议或规划，很难经常性地现场讨论和介绍双方对外合作倡议或规划的对接，很难让两国媒体、商界等一下听到和知晓两国发展倡议或规划是如何对接的，很难让两国商界立即发现对接合作的商机，很难让两国百姓快速了解到支持和参与两国合作的诸多收益。

① 林展霆：《美向印太再投3亿美元明显加强抗衡“一带一路”》，〔新加坡〕《联合早报》网，2018年8月6日，https：//www.zaobao.com/news/china/story20180806－880983。

因此，建议中泰两国未来要更多组织两国官员和专家联合在两国进行巡回式的宣传介绍活动，现场宣传中国“一带一路”倡议与泰国“东部经济走廊”发展规划如何进行对接合作，以及加强合作给两国不同群体带来的诸多收益是什么。这样才能更多赢得两国商界、民众的理解、支持和参与，消除彼此间的误解与疑虑。

在具体操作层面，针对双方的对外合作倡议或规划的对接，两国应该组建一个专门的宣讲团队。这个团队应该由两国的国际问题专家、语言文化专家、经济学家、科技专家、环境专家、媒体人士、民间组织人士等组成，这些专家应该对两国国情非常了解，能经常性地深入两国商界、媒体界、民众间宣传中国“一带一路”倡议与泰国“东部经济走廊”发展规划如何进行对接合作，推动两国不同群体积极参与双方合作中去。

同时，两国政府部门、商界、学界等要更加支持中国华侨大学与泰国国家研究院、泰中文化经济协会等机构联合主办的年度“中泰战略研讨会”更加深入务实地讨论中国“一带一路”倡议与泰国“东部经济走廊”发展规划如何进行对接合作，更加支持参与研讨会的两国专家更多实地考察两国重要发展区域，更加支持两国专家开展联合调研，以便他们能更好地向两国政府提出对接合作的可行性建议。

在未来合作中，中泰都应该更加注意“舒适度”原则。

中国是大国，泰国是中等国家，因此，中泰两国在开展合作时，彼此的思维方式和行为模式自然会有所不同，甚至会因为实力差距、沟通方式等问题而发生一些不悦。因此，双方在开展合作时，未来应该更多理解对方的思维方式和行为习惯，更多倾听对方的诉求，更多去寻找双方的舒适点和利益契合点，减少摩擦。

同时，未来双方要根据形势发展需要，动态调整合作的方式方法、力度、规模等，从而避免双方利益脱节情况以及由此产生的问题，尽量使双方合作能动态地符合双方的利益需求和可承受能力。当双方合作出现分歧和问题时，不能继续强推，而是要调整进度。双方合作要时刻注意效率、舒适度、彼此接受度、可行性等多方面的综合平衡。

双方合作要更加重视民心相通这个领域，要鼓励民众更多参与两国经贸合作，同时也要让双方经贸合作带给民众更多实实在在的获得感，让民众更加支持双方经贸合作。

中泰政府要更多支持两国商人、媒体人士、专家、民间人士等各行各业人士增加交流，重视妥善处理2018年7月5日泰国普吉岛沉船事故造成中国人大量伤亡等影响两国民间交往的重大事件，推动两国民间对彼此形成稳固的积极认知态势。只有两国民间友好情感日益深厚和牢固，才会使两国合作有着更加坚实的民间基础，有着源源不断的民间支持。

中泰两国要加强人力资源合作开发，以满足中国“一带一路”倡议与泰国“东部经济走廊”发展规划对接合作的需要。中泰两国应重视联合培养更多合格的人才，这些人才更多是“语言+专业”的复合型人才，即掌握中泰语言文化，并精通国际关系、跨文化交际、经济学、金融、贸易、某一工业或产业领域的技能、农业或环境等某一个或几个领域的专业知识，更直接、更快捷地服务于中泰经贸合作。

多措并举深入推进澜湄合作

马　勇*

摘　要： 湄公河国家在新时代我国推动形成全面开放新格局中的地位更加凸显，扩大对外开放要重视深化澜湄合作。我国与湄公河国家具有成为命运共同体的天然条件，推动构建澜湄国家命运共同体成为我国构建人类命运共同体的先导；澜沧江－湄公河次区域是“丝绸之路经济带”和“21世纪海上丝绸之路”的交汇地带，湄公河国家是“一带一路”建设的天然伙伴；澜湄合作机制是我国重点投入和打造的周边合作平台，是我国推进周边外交的重要创举，是我国推动与东盟国家关系发展的重要抓手；党的十九大后，习近平主席首次出访就选择了越南、老挝两个湄公河国家，李克强总理出访柬埔寨，王毅外长奉命出访缅甸，传递出我国

* 马勇，云南省社会科学院、中国（昆明）南亚东南亚研究院东南亚研究所所长、研究员。

重视发展与湄公河国家关系发展的明确信号；澜湄合作启动以来一大批务实合作项目开花结果，给湄公河国家人民带来了实实在在的利益，湄公河国家对参与澜湄合作更为积极，对我国有更多期待，推进澜湄合作具有较好的社会和民意基础。我们要顺势而谋，坚持以构建人类命运共同体的先导为目标，以“三感三得”理念为准则，突出重点与整体推进相结合，注重发挥中央和地方两方面积极性，更加积极主动推进澜湄合作，推动构建澜湄国家命运共同体。

开放是国家繁荣发展的必由之路。以开放促改革、促发展，是我国改革开放40年来现代化建设取得巨大成就的重要法宝。党的十九大宣告中国特色社会主义进入了新时代，中国特色社会主义进入新时代，开启了我国同世界交融发展的新画卷。在新时代提升对外开放水平，以“一带一路”建设为重点推动形成全面开放新格局，对于实现“两个一百年”奋斗目标、实现中华民族伟大复兴的中国梦、推动构建人类命运共同体具有重大意义。我国与湄公河国家合作基础好、合作条件佳、合作意愿强、合作潜力大，湄公河国家在新时代中国特色周边外交和“一带一路”建设中的地位更加凸显，扩大开放要重视深化澜湄合作。

一 从中方角度看，构建全面开放新格局需要发挥好澜湄合作的示范作用

第一，我国与湄公河国家具有成为命运共同体的天然条件，推动构建澜湄国家命运共同体成为我国构建人类命运共同体的先导。周边是我国安身立命之所，发展繁荣之基，我国与周边国家同呼吸、共命运。周边好，我国才能发展好；我国发展好，周边会变得更好。我国同湄公河国家山水相连，传统友谊世代相传，是天然的合作伙伴和紧密的友好邻邦。近代以来，在争取国家独立和民族解放的斗争中，我国人民同湄公河国家人民并肩战斗、彼此支援，结下了深厚情谊，为我国同湄公河国家世代友好奠定了坚实基础。中华人民共和国成立以来，我国同湄公河国家关系经受住了时代变迁和国际风云变幻的考验，关系得到长足发展。特别是近年来，我国同湄公河国家都建立了全面战略合作伙伴关系，利益紧密交融，合作基础扎实，我国是柬埔寨、缅甸、泰国和越南的第一大贸易伙伴国，是柬埔寨、老挝和缅甸的第一大投资国，推动构建澜湄国家命运共同体成为我国构建人类命运共同体的先导。①

① 《李克强：携手打造澜湄国家命运共同体》，新华网，2016 年 3 月 23 日，http://www.xinhuanet.com/world/2016-03/23/c_1118421512.htm。

第二，湄公河流域地区是“丝绸之路经济带”和“21世纪海上丝绸之路”的交汇地带，湄公河国家是“一带一路”建设的天然伙伴。湄公河流域地区是古代海上丝绸之路的必经之地，也是“丝绸之路经济带”和“21世纪海上丝绸之路”的交汇地带，参与“一带一路”国际合作条件得天独厚，基础牢固。湄公河国家同我国地缘相近、人文相亲、经济互补，在工业化、基础设施、产业结构升级、农业现代化等方面和我国拥有广泛的合作需求或互补优势，是我国加强各领域合作的天然伙伴，也是我国推进“一带一路”建设和开展国际产能合作的重要对象。

第三，澜湄合作机制是我国重点投入和打造的周边合作平台，是我国推进周边外交的重要创举，是我国推动与东盟国家关系发展的重要抓手。澜湄合作是首个由澜沧江－湄公河流域六国共商、共建、共享的新型次区域合作机制，是我国重点投入和打造的周边合作平台，是我国推进周边外交的重要创举，是我国推动与东盟国家关系发展的重要抓手。2016年3月，澜湄合作首次领导人会议在海南三亚举行，宣告澜湄合作机制正式启动。启动两年多来，澜湄合作机制建设取得重要成果，合作项目稳步落地，资金安排逐步到位，全方位合作态势初步形成，未来合作规划基本成型，澜湄合作正在不断走深走实，澜湄合作正从培育期进入成长期。2018年1月，澜湄合作第二次领导人会议在柬埔寨金边召开，会议主题为“我们的和平与可持续发展之河”，会议发表了《澜湄合作五年行动计划》《澜湄合作第二次领导人会议金边宣言》两份重要合作文件，会议规划了新时代澜湄合作蓝图，开启了澜湄合作新篇章。

第四，党的十九大后，习近平总书记首次出访就选择了越南、老挝两个湄公河国家，传递出我国重视发展与湄公河国家关系发展的明确信号。2017 年 11 月 12 ~ 14 日，习近平主席以中共中央总书记、国家主席双重身份在党的十九大后首访即前往越南、老挝两国，实现中越、中老两党两国最高领导人年内互访，体现对巩固双方睦邻友好、推进全面战略合作的高度重视，向国际社会传递出中国推动构建周边命运共同体的明确信号。访问期间，习近平主席同越南、老挝领导人就巩固政治互信、密切战略沟通、深化党际交往和执政经验交流、加强多边协调、维护共同战略利益达成重要共识，双方全面战略合作伙伴关系迈上了新台阶，务实合作得到新的拓展。习近平主席同两国领导人就密切双边各领域合作做出系统部署和全面规划，同意加快发展战略对接，稳步推进重点合作项目。越南公开支持共建“一带一路”倡议，双方签署“一带一路”和“两廊一圈”建设政府间合作文件，为双方下阶段合作明确努力方向。中老商定以中老铁路为依托共同建设中老经济走廊，成为“一带一路”倡议同老挝“变陆锁国为陆联国”战略对接的最重要成果。

二　从外方角度看，推进澜湄合作具有较好的社会和民意基础

澜湄合作启动以来一大批务实合作项目开花结果，给湄公河国家人民带来了实实在在的利益，澜湄国家各界人士高度评价澜湄合作发挥的作用，对澜湄合作有更多期待。

一是认为澜湄合作发展迅速，成效显著。缅甸副总统吴敏瑞认为，三年前在内比都举办的澜湄合作会议现如今快速发展，成为区域性的合作组织。[①] 越南《人民报》发表的评论说，经过两年的努力，澜湄六国已开展一些具体活动，包括成立水资源、减贫、对接、产能合作联合工作组；开展早期收获合作项目名单中的若干项目，如干部交流计划、人道主义人眼手术项目、妇女合作论坛、湄公河－澜沧江旅游城市合作论坛；将湄公河－澜沧江合作专项基金投入运行；在各自国家成立湄公河－澜沧江合作国家秘书处和协调机关等。[②] 柬埔寨国家科委主席、柬埔寨工业与手工业部副国务秘书邓西尼认为，澜湄机制有助于各国畅所欲言，凝聚共识，他表示："对于区域治理，每个国家都会有各自的想法。但是在澜湄机制的框架

---

① 缅甸《镜报》，2018 年 1 月 10 日。

② 《推动湄公河－澜沧江合作共谋区域繁荣发展》，越南人民报网，2018 年 1 月 10 日，http：//cn. nhandan. org. vn/political/item/5767101。

下，各国代表可以汇聚一堂，共同讨论，凝聚共识。我希望这一机制今后能运行得越来越好。”①

二是认为澜湄流域六国携手合作，对确保地区安全与繁荣至关重要。柬埔寨首相洪森在自己的脸书页面上发文写道：“澜湄六国追求稳定和发展的共同需求，将促进澜湄合作取得‘更加快速的发展’，帮助澜湄地区各国实现共同繁荣的目标。”② 柬埔寨国务兼外交国际合作部大臣布拉索昆认为：“澜沧江-湄公河是澜湄国家的生命之源，澜湄流域六国携手合作，对确保地区安全与繁荣至关重要。”“澜湄国家是地区和全球一体化的支持者，澜湄合作机制是一个务实的机制，能够充分利用澜湄国家地缘相近、人文相通、经济互补的特点，提高在互联互通、产能、跨境经济、水资源、农业和减贫等领域的合作，从而缩小湄公河次区域发展差异，并帮助加快东盟共同体建设。”③ 缅甸天网电视台新闻部总编吴亨拉认为：“相信澜沧江-湄公河合作机制将在经济、文化、水资源、互联互通

① 《柬埔寨官员：澜湄合作机制有助于各国畅所欲言凝聚共识》，国际在线，2018年1月9日，http://news.cri.cn/20180109/66832bc2-db83-ff9b-7278-fad95f6dfa82.html。

② 《李克强柬埔寨之行，外媒热议“澜湄速度”》，中国政府网，2018年1月11日，http://www.gov.cn/guowuyuan/2018-01/11/content_5255667.htm。

③ 《专访：澜湄国家携手合作至关重要——访柬埔寨国务兼外交国际合作部大臣布拉索昆》，新华网，2018年1月11日，http://www.xinhuanet.com/2018-01/11/c_1122246053.htm。

和减贫方面起到重要作用。”《曼谷邮报》评论说，在澜湄领导人第二次会议为期两天的活动中，中国、缅甸、老挝、越南、泰国和柬埔寨的领导人将努力把湄公河转变为和平与可持续发展的河流。澜湄6个国家都达成共识，承诺共同努力，高效务实推进澜湄合作。[①]

三是认为澜湄合作反映了流域国家致力构建命运共同体的共同愿望。缅甸国际合作部部长吴觉丁表示，习近平主席提出了愿同各国人民同心协力构建人类命运共同体的伟大倡议，那么，澜湄国家命运共同体将是推动人类命运共同体建设的先行者，是人类命运共同体的有益补充。[②] 缅甸天网电视台新闻部总编吴亨拉认为，澜湄国家命运共同体是人类命运共同体建设的重要组成部分。他说：“中国国家主席习近平提出的构建‘人类命运共同体’指的是全人类共同发展，尤其是针对一些发展中国家，中国通过合作来帮助这些国家实现共同发展。澜沧江—湄公河命运共同体是构建‘人类命运共同体’中的一部分，构建澜沧江—湄公河命运共同体，将有助于中国与湄公

① 《李克强金边“模拟驾驶”中国高铁澜湄六国合作共谋发展》，环球网，2018年1月11日，http://world.huanqiu.com/exclusive/2018-01/11513471.html。

② 《缅甸国际合作部部长：缅甸为支持澜湄共同体建设提供强大助力》，国际在线，2017年12月15日，http://news.cri.cn/20171215/814013a8-914d-894f-6404-a2f2f5e4253e.html。

河流域五个国家实现共同富裕与和平。”[①] 柬埔寨战略研究所副所长强万纳里说，澜湄合作反映了流域国家致力于实现合作共赢以及建立澜湄国家命运共同体的共同愿望，中国在推动澜湄合作机制发展方面发挥了重要作用。

四是湄公河国家希望在澜湄合作框架下与中国加强多领域、多层次的合作。越南希望同中国和湄公河次区域各国配合展开湄澜水资源合作中心成立项目，以互相分享信息，提高大湄公河水资源可持续管理能力，特别希望推动与中国在经贸、投资领域合作。[②] 缅甸国际合作部部长吴觉丁表示，缅甸在澜湄合作中有着更多的机遇，缅甸将继续深入和澜湄各国在经济贸易、项目投资等领域的合作，将“一带一路”与澜湄合作联系起来。缅甸天网电视台新闻部总编吴亨拉表示非常期待今后“澜湄合作”专项基金能为缅甸电力与交通发展提供帮助。“国家经济发展需要吸引投资，吸引外来投资首先就是确保电力供应，我认为缅中还应就电力发展进行合作，尤其是水力发电，无论是小型水电站还是中型水电站，只有尽快实现通电才能为企业发展提供环境，促进当地经济发展，提高人民生活水平。其次就是交通，在‘澜湄合作’中互联互通也是优先发

① 《缅甸资深媒体人坚定看好“澜湄合作”认为媒体应发挥积极宣传作用》，中国政府网，2018 年 1 月 10 日，http://www.gov.cn/xinwen/2018－01/10/content_5255130.htm。

② 越通社，2018 年 1 月 8 日。

展的一个领域。"[1] 缅甸《镜报》报道，澜湄合作框架下的事项的精髓就在于实现地区的发展与和平，最基本的是让人民生活富足。缅甸将会继续努力和湄公河流域国家共同协商、互信解决自己国家面临的经济、社会、环境等的挑战和恐怖主义。柬埔寨国家科委主席、柬埔寨工业与手工业部副国务秘书邓西尼指出，柬埔寨正在推进"2015～2025 工业发展计划"，这一计划契合中国的"一带一路"倡议。中国的"一带一路"倡议将给柬埔寨的发展带来诸多好处："柬埔寨坚定支持'一带一路'倡议。'一带一路'倡议强调互联互通，让沿线国家经济更加开放。同时，包括柬埔寨在内的东盟国家也能够通过'一带一路'了解中国在科技方面的成就。中国向柬埔寨提供了技术援助，北斗卫星示范系统在柬埔寨落地揭牌。中国还支持柬埔寨派遣学生和官员到中国学习先进技术，培养柬埔寨科技方面的人才。这有助于柬埔寨借鉴中国先进经验并实现自身发展。"[2] 泰国《曼谷邮报》发表的评论说，中国在澜湄合作问题上所发挥的作用为确保全流域有效合作并制定更明确的程序来保证对该区域的可持续管理创造了机遇。虽然水治理是澜

---

① 《缅甸资深媒体人坚定看好"澜湄合作"认为媒体应发挥积极宣传作用》，中国政府网，2018 年 1 月 10 日，http：//www. gov. cn/xinwen/2018 －01/10/content_ 5255130. htm。

② 《柬埔寨官员：澜湄合作机制有助于各国畅所欲言凝聚共识》，国际在线，2018 年 1 月 9 日，http：//news. cri. cn/20180109/66832bc2 － db83 －ff9b －7278 －fad95f6dfa82. html。

湄合作的关键目标，不过它所涵盖的领域要比湄公河委员会宽泛得多，拓展至跨境投资和减少贫困等区域合作，让加大对水力发电及基建项目决策影响力成为一种可能，泰国希望在这些方面与中国加强合作。[①]

三 新时代推进澜湄合作的几点思考

（一）坚持以构建人类命运共同体为共同愿景

人类命运共同体理念是全球治理中国方案的灵魂，推动构建人类命运共同体是新时代中国特色大国外交的目标，其主要任务就是要建设一个持久和平、普遍安全、共同繁荣、开放包容、清洁美丽的世界。人类命运共同体理论是习近平总书记深刻洞察世界大势，准确把握时代脉搏，既立足中国，又放眼全球；既立足当前，又心系未来，回应国际社会的共同期待，站在国际道义制高点上提出的重大理论，它科学地回答了“建设一个什么样的世界、怎么样建设世界”的重大历史命题。澜湄国家命运共同体建设是对习近平总书记提出的推动构建人类命运共同体的具体实践，澜湄国家命运共同体建设已成为我国构建人类命运共同体的先导，而打造中越、中老、中柬具有

① 《地区合作能否确保湄公河的未来?》,《曼谷邮报》2018 年 1 月 10 日。

战略意义的命运共同体，把湄公河国家摆到了突出位置。

构建澜湄国家命运共同体是首个得到相关国家正式认可且已进入建设议程的命运共同体。2016 年 3 月 23 日，首次澜湄合作领导人会议在海南三亚举行。我国同湄公河国家领导人一致同意秉持共商、共建、共享原则，对接发展战略，统筹合作资源，共享发展成果，共建团结互助、平等协商、互利互惠、合作共赢的澜湄国家命运共同体。2017 年 12 月 15 日，澜湄合作第三次外长会在云南大理举行。王毅外长同湄公河国家外长高度评价澜湄合作启动一年半以来取得的显著进展，指出全方位合作态势初步形成，未来合作规划基本成型，各方将致力于打造澜湄流域经济发展带，共建澜湄国家命运共同体。推进澜湄合作要围绕共建团结互助、平等协商、互利互惠、合作共赢的澜湄国家命运共同体，坚持以构建人类命运共同体的先导为目标，为在更广范围内构建亚洲命运共同体打下坚实的基础。

（二）以“三感三得”理念推进澜湄合作

推进澜湄合作需要树立正确的理念，反思我国与湄公河国家合作的经验教训，宜以“三感三得”理念推进澜湄合作。“三感”是指在与湄公河国家的交往中，让湄公河国家有被尊重感、认同感和获得感。湄公河国家都是中小国家，一些国家还具有浓厚的民族主义传统，对是否被尊重看得很重，因此，在推动与湄公河国家合作中要注意尊重他们。多措并举，精准发力，让命运共同体意识在湄公河国家落地生根，让湄公河国家人民对推进澜湄合作、构建澜湄国家命运共同体有认同感，彼此关照各方利益，实现互利共赢。在具体的项目合作中让湄公河国家人民有获得感，反思以往我国湄公河国家尤其是在缅甸投资项目的成败，可以发现，民众的"获得感"是影响中国在湄公河国家投资项目成败的重要变量。同样，民众的"获得感"也将在很大程度上影响未来我国与湄公河国家的合作。顺利推进我国与湄公河国家的合作，既需要关注湄公河国家的发展需求，也不能忽视民众的"获得感"。"三得"是指考虑到湄公河国家国情和文化的特点，推进与湄公河国家合作总体急不得；但具体合作项目，尤其是早期收获项目推进慢不得；落实国家推动与湄公河国家合作战略任务和处理合作中的纠纷等不得。

（三）多边与双边相结合推进我国与湄公河国家的合作

推进澜湄合作，构建澜湄国家命运共同体，呼唤正确理念的引领，更需凝聚行动的力量。要围绕"一带一路"在湄公河流域地区顺利推进为主要任务，以多边引导双边，双边促进多边的方式推进我国与湄公河国家的合作。在多边层面，要结合《澜沧江—湄公河合作五年行动计划（2018～2022）》，着力推进澜湄流域经济发展带建设，推动澜湄合作，始终把发展作为优先方向，致力于把经济互补性转化为发展互助力，打造发展中国家携手合作、共谋发展的样板，尊重文化多样化，以文明互鉴超越文明冲突、文明共存超越文明优越，实现澜湄流域文化发展振兴。双边层面，要贯彻落实好我国同湄公河国家达成的重要共识，推动“一带一路”倡议与湄公河国家发展战略和发展规划对接，尤其是要推动中越、中老、中缅经济走廊建设，适时启动中老泰经济走廊、中老柬经济走廊、中缅孟经济走廊建设，推进“21 世纪海上丝绸之路”和南方丝绸之路经济带的有机对接和衔接。

（四）注重发挥中央和地方两方面积极性

推进我国与湄公河国家的合作，既要注重从国家层面予以推进，又要重视发挥好地方的积极性，尤其要重视发挥好云南的独特作用。云南与越南、老挝、缅甸 3 个国家接壤，边境线 4061 公里，与泰国和柬埔寨通过澜沧江 - 湄公河相连，是我国面向湄公河国家开放的关键枢纽，云南与湄公河国家的国际区域合作成为我国区域合作中最富成效的重要组成部分。澜湄合作起源于云南，至今召开的三次外长会议，两次在云南举行，足见云南在澜湄合作中的分量。为充分发挥云南在我国与湄公河国家合作的独特作用，可以考虑在云南建立澜湄合作国际秘书处，有效降低协调成本。为此，中央可从四个方面支持云南。

一是支持云南建设沿边自由贸易试验区。自由贸易试验区是新形势下我国推进开放的重要平台，国家已经先后启动三批十一个自由贸易试验区建设，从区域布局来看，主要集中在沿海地区和长江经济带。云南具有从陆上沟通太平洋和印度洋，连接南亚、东亚和东南亚三大市场的桥梁和纽带作用，是我国走向印度洋的重要通道，在“一带一路”建设中具有重要地位。“一带一路”建设中优先推进的六大多边经济走廊，有两大经济走廊，即中国－中南半岛经济走廊和孟中印缅经济走廊，中老、中缅两条双边经济走廊，云南都是主体省份，云南理应承担国家对外开放的重大责任。在云南设立沿边自由贸易试验区，对于促进“一带一路”从战略概念转变为网格化周边共同体具有重要意义和作用。在云南建立沿边自贸试验区，可以把中国开放前沿向南亚和东南亚的腹地前移，大大缩短中国内地市场与东南亚－南亚市场的空间距离和体制差距。

二是支持云南开展边民互市贸易改革升级试点。允许建立边民互助组织，鼓励“互市＋加工”模式，使互市进口商品变穿岸而过为落地加工，变“通道经济”为“产业经济”，延伸产业链，提高附加值。允许云南沿边县符合条件的边民互助合作组织以集体形式开展互市贸易。对边民互助组实施政府和海关、检验检疫共同备案制度。开设边民互助合作组专用申报窗口，优先办理边民互助合作组业务；允许边民互助合作组申请预约通关，视情况可适当延长通关时间；允许同一边民互助合作组申报的货物拼车运输，降低运输成本；对边民互助合作组实行分类评级管理。

三是支持云南开展非传统安全区域合作试验示范。提高边防管控和出入境管理能力和技术装备水平，切实做好周边外事、侨务及出入境管理工作。在地区贫困、恐怖主义、流行疾病、走私贩毒、非法移民等非传统安全领域，搭建周边对话磋商平台，培育地区安全合作架构，巩固和提升云南影响周边、引领周边、塑造周边的地位和作用。

四是实施云南对外交往能力提升工程。由国家相关部委和云南省联合编制《云南对外交往能力提升计划》，启动实施云南对外交往能力提升工程，通过实施一系列重要项目，着力提升云南教育、科技、文化、卫生、科研、青年、妇女等机构的自我发展能力和对外交往能力，支持云南高校启动国门大学建设，支持云南智库机构和高校加强对澜湄合作深度研究。

图书在版编目（CIP）数据

中国－东盟命运共同体与澜湄合作：第九届西南论坛暨第二届澜湄合作智库论坛论文集 / 林文勋，郑永年主编. --北京：社会科学文献出版社，2019.8
ISBN 978-7-5201-5309-6

Ⅰ.①中… Ⅱ.①林… ②郑… Ⅲ.①自由贸易区-区域经济发展-中国、东南亚国家联盟-学术会议-文集 ②湄公河-流域-国际合作-区域经济合作-文集 Ⅳ.①F752.733-53 ②D822.333-53

中国版本图书馆 CIP 数据核字（2019）第 160436 号

中国－东盟命运共同体与澜湄合作
——第九届西南论坛暨第二届澜湄合作智库论坛论文集

主　　编 / 林文勋　郑永年

出 版 人 / 谢寿光
组稿编辑 / 宋月华　周志静
责任编辑 / 周志静

出　　版 / 社会科学文献出版社 · 人文分社（010）59367215
地址：北京市北三环中路甲 29 号院华龙大厦　邮编：100029
网址：www.ssap.com.cn
发　　行 / 市场营销中心（010）59367081　59367083
印　　装 / 三河市龙林印务有限公司

规　　格 / 开 本：787mm×1092mm　1/16
印 张：16　字 数：154 千字
版　　次 / 2019 年 8 月第 1 版　2019 年 8 月第 1 次印刷
书　　号 / ISBN 978-7-5201-5309-6
定　　价 / 89.00 元